M000011349

A Guide to Getting It:

Creative Intelligence

Deborah Gordon Bernstein • Kathryn Bonner
Denise Braunstein • Wendi Kovar
Ted Prodromou • Nova Reed
Marilyn Schwader • Gwen Thelen
Lydia Van den Broeck
Aline Vieira • Laura Young

Marilyn Schwader, Editor

CLARITY OF VISION PUBLISHING • PORTLAND, OREGON

Other books in the series:
A Guide to Getting It: Self-Esteem
A Guide to Getting It: Achieving Abundance
A Guide to Getting It: Remarkable Management Skills
A Guide to Getting It: A Clear, Compelling Vision
A Guide to Getting It: Powerful Leadership Skills
A Guide to Getting It: Sacred Healing
A Guide to Getting It: Purpose & Passion

For more information, visit www.ClarityOfVision.com
To order any of the *A Guide to Getting It* book series,
visit www.ClarityOfVision.com/webstore.htm

BOOK DESIGN AND PRODUCTION BY MARILYN SCHWADER

ISBN 0-9716712-7-3
Library of Congress Control Number: 2006927592
First edition: July 2006

Table of Contents

Acknowledgments

With heartfelt gratitude, I would like to honor all of the wonderful people in my life who have supported and encouraged my creative endeavors. From the seed of inspiration, you have helped me manifest the idea for this book into an extraordinary tool for healing. Thank you to my dear friends who continue to provide incredible insights for my growth. You are in my life for reasons beyond our understanding. To my coaches, who have helped me attain so much by reflecting honesty and authenticity, I am truly indebted. To my family, who have provided amazing love through a difficult time, I am profoundly thankful. And especially, to the authors who have contributed their expertise and talents to the writing of this book. Your courage, trust, and inspiration have been tremendous. I am so fortunate to be able to work with such forward thinking souls.

Marilyn Schwader, Editor

A Note from the Editor

The chapters in this book combine years of coaching experience with lifetimes of personal experience in the collected works of eleven Life and Business Coaches. Wherever you are in terms of creativity and living your life from source, these authors have been there. Whether you are an artist trying to overcome a creative block, facing challenges in your business, or looking for a way to have more ease in your life, this book will help you understand how awareness, beliefs, and choice affect what you create. Through their stories and perspectives, the authors guide you to break down barriers and reconnect with your true nature. Apply the lessons told here, and you will enhance your Creative Intelligence, no matter what you are bringing into being.

This unique guide will give you access to powerful, life-changing insights, examples, and exercises to help you discover—or rediscover—your Creative Intelligence.

This book is the eighth in a series of books written by Life and Business Coaches to help the reader improve their business and personal life. I invite you to read, explore, become aware, and change how you feel about creating.

Marilyn Schwader, Editor

The Energy of Emotion:
Connecting With Creative Intelligence

By Marilyn Schwader

The phone woke me early that morning. I let it ring, thinking that it must be either a wrong number or one of my clients forgetting the three-hour difference in time from the east coast. The clock read 5:36 a.m. I rolled over, hoping to catch a few more minutes of sleep before getting up for the day. When the phone rang again less than a minute later, I felt a nervous panic rise in my body. Something didn't feel right, now that I was awake. I stumbled into the hallway, and hurried to the phone in my office.

When I answered, my brother's voice was on the other end of the line. Knowing Tony, the time of day, and the urgency in his hello, something serious had happened.

"Mom died last night," he said, ignoring my greeting to him. The air rushed from my lungs, my legs felt weak, and my half-asleep brain stumbled.

"What did you say?" I replied angrily, as if he had told me a cruel joke.

"Mom died last night," he repeated, surreally calm in the face of my anger and the devastating news he was conveying.

What he was telling me could not be true. Trudy Schwader was one of the most healthy and active women of her age that I knew. She had never taken the medications that others her age seemed to rely on. She didn't have diabetes, or high blood pressure, or any of a number of other maladies overcoming her aging siblings. She had just celebrated her 76th birthday earlier that month, and had been visiting my sister to celebrate my nephew's third birthday. After spending most of her 50 years of marriage to my father caring for him during his many surgeries and protracted years of Parkinson's, she was "sewing and going", making quilts, traveling the world, enjoying life. This was either a huge mistake or she had been in a terrible accident.

"What happened?" I demanded, as if the knowledge of that would somehow change the reality of what I was hearing.

In my brother's own way of bringing lightness to the moment, he replied again, "Well... she died."

Later, when he told me that calling all of his siblings was a blur, that he didn't remember much of the conversations, I reminded him of his reply. He said that he knew I would be able to handle his attempt to lighten the conversation. That was true; I had actually smiled at what he said that morning, knowing it was his way of handling his grief.

Our family is very close. I'm one of eight siblings who grew up on a farm on the South Dakota plains. My mother's heart attack and death cut deeply through my immediate family, and caused severe ripples through the layers of the large clan that is my extended family.

The rest of that day was spent talking with my other siblings, making plans for the trip home for the funeral, receiving calls from relatives and friends, washing clothes, and packing. Like the Zen saying, "first enlightenment, then the laundry"; in this case, first death....

So much can change in a moment. On the flight back to South Dakota, I looked back at how my life had been before Tony's call. In the two months leading up to Mom's death, I had been reading a book by Esther and Jerry Hicks titled, *Ask and It Is Given: Learning to Manifest Your Desires*. In it, Esther Hicks channels the teachings of Abraham, a collective voice of her spiritual guides.

The basic principle of the book is that each of us is born with an innate knowledge that we create our own reality. This knowledge is so fundamental that when you or someone you know attempts to stop you from creating, you feel immediate conflict within yourself. You are the creator of your own experience, and ultimately that creation is absolutely and entirely up to you. The book describes how to realign with Source Energy, God—what I call Creative Intelligence. The name does not matter; the source is the same.

When you are joyfully allowing your true nature to flow through you, Creative Intelligence is expressed and reflected by what you create, be it a piece of art, a business, or your life. By consciously choosing your thoughts, you maintain a continuous, loving connection with that divine source of energy.

When you allow your thoughts to move away from your true nature, the channel to that Creative Intelligence is affected, and so will the outcome of what you create. The resulting energy that you attract into your life will be less than spectacular, and sometimes horrible because it does not match the joyous and loving energy of the divine source. This simple concept is so easily shoved aside in our hectic, societal-influenced lives.

Because of my work, I am continually learning about creativity, resulting in a desire to explore the topic of what I call Creative Intelligence. When I started to delve into the subject, I was thinking about the creative *process* versus the idea of it being a source of energy. The realization that began to form was that the flow of life and what is referred to as the "creative flow" are the same processes. The only difference is the scale of the outcome. Getting "into the flow" requires an ability to be in the moment, to set your ego-brain aside and allow the energy to move through you without limits or blocks. Doing that, you connect with Source Energy in a joyous state that creates unlimited potential. You are in your true nature. Regardless of the size of the creation (a painting, a business, or your life), the result of being in flow will be a work of art.

This, I saw, was what Abraham-Hicks was describing. Their writing explained how to easily know when you are connected to that divine source, and how to get there if you are not.

In the two months I had been studying the book, the personal and professional parts of my life expanded considerably. The night before Mom died, I was ready to launch two new products, my marketing efforts had been successful, and I was feeling joy like I hadn't in years. I had written my chapter for *Creative Intelligence*, and was scheduled to start production of this book that week.

Then the phone call came. I stuck *Ask and It Is Given* into my carrying case and flew home for the funeral. Although I brought the book out onto my nightstand of the guest room in the house we were all staying, I did not read any of it. The message of joy the book carried was eluding me in my sorrow. Unbeknownst to me, my brother and two sisters were at that time also studying Esther Hicks and the teachings of Abraham. When they saw the book, they had a long and spirited conversation about the topic of manifesting thoughts. I quietly listened, not sure how everything fit together anymore.

I was the last out-of-state sibling to leave after the funeral services, and had the house to myself the evening before my flight. All day I had looked forward to the quiet that had eluded me during ten days of grieving, visiting relatives, and trying to wake myself up from what seemed like a bad dream. When I opened the door to the now-empty house, I suddenly had a feeling of claustrophobia, of my breath being sucked out of me. I busied myself with packing, desperately wishing for company, when I heard a vehicle pull up. Tony, who was driving to his home two miles away stopped by to see if I wanted company. He was the answer to my prayers. We talked for hours about beliefs, death and life, creating our reality, and joy.

He asked me how, if Abraham-Hicks's book was correct, we had created the reality of Mom's death. That was the question I had held in my mind since their discovery of the book on my nightstand. I thought about it for a moment, then replied that it wasn't that we had manifested her death, but that perhaps we had manifested what we were looking to learn from her passing. The learning would be different for each of us. What I suggested we do was to focus on the joy of what Mom had brought to our lives, of the good that would come from our collective grief and support. Because based on what I had been discovering in my work and experience, if we focused on the bad, we would be inviting more of it into our lives.

As I finished packing in the early morning hours, I stuck the book in my case, and promptly forgot about it, not reading another word. And my advice to my brother? Somehow that got lost in the cloud of despair I settled into on my return to Portland.

Months passed as I struggled with the grief. Work came to a standstill. Mom had been one of my most steadfast supporters in my life. Her loss was huge. Fortunately, I work with coaches and there was incredible support and patience as I worked my way through the heaviness. The months were a blur. There were flashes of motivation, but through the next six months, I staggered in my work, my relationships, and my view of life. I am so grateful for my family, friends, and clients who were there to support me as I moved through that feeling of anguish and overwhelm.

Shortly before Thanksgiving, my brother and I had another conversation. We were dealing with the emotions of the holidays without Mom. Like me, he had continued to question the meaning of life in face of our tremendous loss. The talk turned to that long-forgotten book by Abraham-Hicks. He had begun to read it again, and had found some relief in the words and the exercises in the book. It reminded me that I hadn't read any more of it since I had returned from South Dakota. After I hung up the phone, I immediately went to the suitcase in the closet, and after searching the pockets, discovered that the book was still there. I began to devour it, reading half of the book before I put it down later that night. As I read the messages again and started doing the exercises, my reality began to change, almost immediately.

The steps were small at first, but with each re-reading of the book's significant chapters, I saw day-by-day progress as I pulled myself out of the energetic space in which my mind had taken up residence. Ironically, the book addressed both that state, and why I was in it: "The reason you have not already gotten what you desire is because you are holding yourself in a vibrational holding pattern that does not match the vibration of your desire…if you will stop and think about it, or more important, stop and *feel* about it, you can identify your very discord." The book recommended gently releasing my resistant, low-vibration thoughts, and replacing them with ever-increasing thoughts of happiness and joy.

For years, I had been given a message through my life experiences, the people I attracted into my life, and my own intuition. The message seemed simple, and yet I resisted. After reading the book, an understanding started to take form. The message is that to really understand how to operate in this life, I must move back to choosing my direction based on how I *feel*, instead of operating from a place of ego and faulty belief systems adopted from others. For me to change my life I would have to learn—actually re-learn—how to sense the emotion that I was having and change it to attract more of what I desired.

What I had done for large parts of my life was to make choices based on perceived outcomes, largely based on three reasons: safety, approval/acceptance, and control. These reasons all result from living in a state of fear. Fear can be good, when it's in an instinctive situation that keeps us from harm. However, when we operate from that place all of the time, the result is that we create an energy field that brings to our reality more reasons to have fear. The law of attraction is very clear: Whether you think good thoughts or bad thoughts, they will attract the same energy as you give them.

This is true because the energy of your emotion resonates with like energy. Imagine that you enter a room filled with tuning forks of every key on the musical scale. You pick up a C tuning fork and hit it against your hand. The resulting energy of sound that reverberates through the room will cause all of the C tuning forks to resonate. The other forks remain silent. Like attracts like, no matter what form the energy appears.

Emotions are the tuning forks of your life. They are both vehicles and interpreters of energy. They send out energy, and receive like energy. By paying attention to the signals of your emotions, you can gauge the strength or weakness of your connection to Creative Intelligence, the Source Energy. The better you feel, the more you are in connection; the worse you feel, the less you are allowing the connection.

Thoughts and emotions are intrinsically linked: Thoughts stimulate emotion; emotion impacts thought. Even if you are not happy, when you move your mind to memories of happy occasions or to imagine pictures of being joyful, your emotion will begin to change. Conversely, if you experience an emotion, you begin to have thoughts about the cause of that emotion, because you desire to have either more or less of it.

You get what you think, and the subsequent emotion, whether you want it or not. If the majority of your thinking and resulting emotion is focused on the things you desire, your life experience will reflect those thoughts and emotions. If they are focused on scarcity, lack, and fear, you will experience their reflection. Nothing happens in life without your inviting it to you.

How powerful is this idea? A few weeks after I re-read the book, I was driving with my sister Judith on Mt. Hood to go snowshoeing. My two dogs rode in the canopy of my pickup truck.

As we drove, the conversation moved to the approaching five-year mark since a major car accident, in which I had rolled a pickup almost identical to the one I was driving several times before coming to land with the passenger side down and me dangling from the driver's seat belt. We talked for several minutes before she suggested that we might not want to focus on that, since we both believe that we manifest our thoughts and emotions. We laughed about it at the time.

That led to more conversation about what had been manifesting in our lives, and what we wanted to bring in next. I joked that what I wanted to manifest was a new car.

At that point, we hit a stretch of ice. I slowed down, but without warning, my truck suddenly swerved. We crossed the middle line into oncoming traffic, narrowly avoiding several cars.

We slid toward the opposite ditch, the truck twirling180-degrees. As we hit the steep embankment on the other side of the ditch, we flipped over, landing on the passenger side, with me dangling from the seat belt. The significance was not lost on either of us. My mind was reeling with memories and anger. I could not believe that I was once again in *exactly* the same position, and that we had just been talking about it and how we needed to be careful not to manifest it! It was like a bad dream.

After crawling out of the cab in a state of déja vü, I went to check on the dogs and was told by the witnesses to the accident that they had jumped out and taken off in two different directions.

As Judith waited for a tow truck, I strapped on my snowshoes and began to search for Rudy. I found his tracks in the fresh snow and followed them, winding in circles, around and around, up and down steep cliffs and ravines.

As I called for him, I became angrier, as frustration over the missing dogs added another layer of emotion. After about 45 minutes of following his circling path, I realized that staying where I was emotionally would not result in an outcome that I wanted. I had just experienced a huge example of how easily thoughts can manifest; I needed to make it work in my search for the dogs.

I sat down on a large tree stump, breathed deep, and attempted to change my thoughts, in the hope that it would make me feel better and change the energy I was spewing out into the universe. I was clearly operating in the lower level emotions of despair, anger, and frustration. But to be honest, I couldn't see my emotions moving to joy and love in one giant leap. That was too much of a jump. What I could do was make a conscious decision to move to the only emotion I could think of that was more positive than what I was feeling. I thought of doubt, but that didn't seem like a helpful emotion either. Then I remembered optimism. Yes, I could *think* optimistic thoughts, even though I wasn't feeling it just yet.

I began to imagine what it would feel like to find both dogs, how happy I'd be, how excited they'd be, and how joyful the outcome would feel. Gradually, the thought became my emotion, and my spirits lifted.

I decided that I should move back toward the scene of the accident, that Rudy was no longer on the side of the highway that I was looking or he would have responded to my calling for him. As I came closer to my overturned vehicle being pulled from the ditch by the tow truck, Judith came running from the other direction.

"I've found Rudy. He won't come to me, but he's this way!" I followed her and saw that he was hiding behind a bush, trembling with fear. When he realized it was me, he came to me, tail hesitantly wagging, with obvious relief that he was going to be okay.

Bella's return was another story. We searched for the next

several hours, with me reminding myself of my emotions, to stay in that place of optimism. Darkness set in and we agreed to suspend our search for the night. Judith's husband drove us back to their house as I called my friends in Portland and asked them all to send loving energy to Bella, as she was probably very frightened, cold, and hungry, and would appreciate everyone's support.

I also called an energy healer who works with animals. We talked for two hours, using muscle testing, visualizing an outcome, and coming to an emotional state of belief that I would find her. I imagined that she had found a tree well that provided her with shelter in the cold, and that being the very intelligent dog that she was, she would be alive and well in the morning when we came to look for her.

The last place she had been spotted was at a Sno-Park near a road that intersected with the main highway. The road had been closed due to the snow. I pictured finding her on that road, with her running up to me, full of life and smiling (she does that when she's happy). I fell asleep that night sure in the knowledge that we would find her the next morning.

When we arrived at the Sno-Park the next morning, I strapped on the snowshoes again and headed through the trees to the road I had imagined in my mind the night before. I called her name in the quietness of the early morning. Rudy was with me, running in and out of the forest as I walked up the road. There was a fresh layer of snow, and new tracks that looked like those of a small dog. My hopes rose even more.

After traveling for about a quarter mile, Rudy perked up. He headed into the forest, whimpering and running back and forth between me and what was causing his excitement. I started calling her name. Something made me turn around, and running as fast as she could up the road toward us was Bella, covered with a light dusting of snow. The scene was exactly as I had pictured it: she was smiling and overjoyed to see us. I grabbed her in my arms and rolled with her in the snow, both dogs jumping on me, on each other, and running in circles around me.

When I talked with my friends later, nearly all of them had

envisioned the same thing I had, with Bella in the safety of the tree, and running up to me in the morning, smiling and joyous. We had all helped create the happy ending.

The accident reminded me again how much can change in a moment, and that in each of the moments that follow, I can choose to focus on the good instead of the bad. What I also realized was that solutions to questions and problems come to me with much more clarity when I stay present with what is happening within me. When I am able to feel my emotions, my connection with Creative Intelligence is engaged and I know if I'm aligned with that Source Energy or if there is dissonance. If what I feel is a low-vibration emotion, especially related to fear, I stop, breathe, touch the earth, and then determine the emotion I can move to from where I am.

The learning that was reinforced for me this past year is profound, and really quite simple: Life happens in each instant. Each moment provides us with a new choice. And each choice leads us to new possibilities in the next moment. We create our future in each new instant.

What I've also learned is that the thought that brings the most immediate response of positive emotion is that of gratitude. When I am truly grateful for what I have in my life, I feel instantly joyful and more abundance comes to me.

As I began to focus on the new year, I determined to choose joy in every possible way, to embrace all of last year's many challenges as another step in my understanding of Creative Intelligence. The past three months have reflected those moments of choice. On a daily basis, there are phenomenal results. I now know that being very clear about my desires while maintaining high-vibration emotions brings me exactly what I focus on. The more I do it, the easier it is to stay in that vibrational place. I no longer think about what I don't have. I look at what I do have, am grateful for its presence in my life, and look forward with joy to what is coming to me next. The people, activities, and things that appear in my life are proof that I truly am able to create the life I want to live, that my connection to Creative Intelligence is thriving, and that my emotions are resonating with joy and love.

About
Marilyn Schwader

As a Writing and Life Coach, Marilyn Schwader uses humor, compassion, and a strong sense of a writer's abilities to support and motivate her clients to become published authors. She has found that her purpose in life is to give a voice to subjects that benefit others. Her mission is to provide truthful, clear, and motivating information to those who passionately desire more in their lives. Her vision is to use her two passions—coaching and storytelling—to convey this information to as many people as possible.

Marilyn graduated from Oregon State University in Corvallis, Oregon with a Bachelor of Science degree in Technical Journalism with emphasis in Business Management. After working for several years as a technical writer contracting to high tech companies in the United States and Pacific Rim countries, she veered from the writing path and started her first business, M's Tea & Coffee House, in Corvallis.

Five years and numerous disastrous business mistakes later, she left the restaurant business and a short time later discovered coaching. In 1998 she enrolled in Coach University and started Clarity of Vision, Inc., a Business and Life Coaching practice. The law of attraction soon worked its magic, and her talents and experience in writing soon began drawing writing clients to her business.

During this time, Marilyn undertook a three-year project to compile and publish a book about her mother's family history. From that experience, she began helping people self-publish their books. Looking for a way to combine her coaching and writing experience, Marilyn decided to create a book series that would be written by coaches and that highlighted principles and ideas supported in the coaching process.

Thus, the *A Guide to Getting It* book series was born. *A Guide to Getting It: Creative Intelligence* is the eighth book in the series. The first seven books are:

A Guide to Getting It: Self-Esteem

A Guide to Getting It: Achieving Abundance

A Guide to Getting It: Remarkable Management Skills

A Guide to Getting It: A Clear, Compelling Vision

A Guide to Getting It: Powerful Leadership Skills

A Guide to Getting It: Sacred Healing

A Guide to Getting It: Purpose & Passion

Visit www.ClarityOfVision.com for more information about Clarity of Vision, Inc. To contact Marilyn, email Marilyn@ClarityofVision.com or call 503-460-0014.

Let's Get Naked!
Learning to Embrace
Your Inner Clive Barker

By Laura Young

And then I heard myself say, "I'll be right back, I have to go downstairs to get the aliens." I may have been the only one on the planet that day, uttering those words in the middle of making a Christmas gingerbread village.

And the Children Shall Lead Us, If Only We Would Let Them ...

Monique and I began our tradition eleven years ago when she was five years old. What started as a pinch hit baby-sitting favor for her grandmother has continued long past the age I expected her to call it quits because it was no longer "cool." It has even continued despite the fact that she can drive now and surely can find other activities with her teenaged friends. And this is a great kid we are talking about. She has *lots* of friends and is involved in too many activities to list here. Making gingerbread with me is not her only option.

But, I'm the one who has the aliens and this is no ordinary tradition.

Monique and I were in our second or third year of cookie baking when an adult friend of mine came to join us. As was our tradition, I had made every color of dough I could: green, yellow, red, orange, blue, and purple. We made tie-died stars, little purple men, and a long, multicolored snake with the last bit of dough. The sprinkles were flying and it looked as though a sugar bomb had exploded in my kitchen. We were in heaven! At least I thought we were, but it turns out my friend was in agony.

"I couldn't believe how patient you were! I mean, you let her make purple Christmas trees and green dogs! I'd let her do a few of those and then I'd say, 'Okay, that's enough of that, now we have to make some nice ones.' "

I could hear Harry Chapin in my head, *"Flowers are red and green grass is green. There is no need to see flowers any other way than the way they always have been seen."*

Eleven years later, Monique and I still make purple men and, yes, our gingerbread village sports aliens, rubber lizards, miniature princess Barbies, a butler, and zebras in one of the houses. And, no adults are invited to join us.

Fast forward to this Christmas and a visit to another friend's house where the children are intently focused on their craft project. The room is spotless.

"I had such high hopes. In my mind these were perfect." She spoke these words apologetically, with a hint of embarrassment as we watched her four-year-old daughter paint Christmas ornaments. She was making a pink snow man (her favorite color) as her mother winced and fought the urge to hand her a paintbrush dipped in white.

This is how it begins.

I have no intention of vilifying anyone, least of all parents. I will grant you, I don't have kids myself and maybe I just don't understand the stress of having little creativity machines running around all day. The fact is, our creative wounds can come from anywhere and those who deliver them would likely be mortified if they really understood what they were doing.

So, What's the Big Deal? It's Not Like You Can Make a Living As An Artist!

The result of these early creative wounds is not only that we miss the opportunity to discover we are the next Rembrandt or Andy Warhol, or Carly Simon. The damage is much more insidious, as in adulthood we lose our ability to play.

This point was brought home to me by accident. I am blessed to be married to a man who was creatively encouraged as a child. After fifteen years in his presence, one might say my own creative wounds have been healed and I've become uninhibited as a result. Over time, our home, a wonderland of paint effects in a stunning array of colors, had accumulated an impressive array of remnant paints. Desperate to reclaim storage space, I set out to use up as much paint as possible in our laundry room. While painting the unfinished sheet rock white, my husband came in and encouraged me to expand my vision. Patting the conduit for the cold air return he said, "This could be painted, too." With all the permission I needed, I opened color after color and started to play.

My mother called the next day as I was starting on the cabinets. I said, "Come over and make some art with me." That afternoon, she arrived with her sister. I handed each a paintbrush and a cabinet door. That's when I saw it. The deer-in-the-headlights look as out poured the protestations. "I can't draw. I don't know how to paint. I haven't done this since kindergarten…"

"Well, I'm not really giving you a choice. Here are all the colors. Just make something for God's sake, it's a *laundry room!* Worst case scenario is that your first one doesn't turn out the way you like and we paint it over so you can start again. That uses even more paint. Everyone wins!"

I am one of those people who is quite comfortable with other people's unease. I resisted every temptation to let them off the hook and simply waited them out. The only way out of my house was through a painted door.

The Turning Point: Allowing Creative Immersion

If I could bottle what came next, I would. There was a turning point when the resistance gave way and my mother and aunt immersed themselves in the task. My aunt literally did so, tracing her hands on the door, along with the words, "Help, I'm being held prisoner!" That wasn't the remarkable part. Their relationship with what they were creating is what intrigued me. Both were very deliberate about the colors they used. It wasn't that the colors had a conscious meaning or rationale; it was that there was an internally mediated surety about the choice. I could see these moments burst forth, like popcorn. I saw it in their postures as they fell silent. Scanning the colors, moving a brush toward one, hesitating, then relaxing as the brush headed to a different hue, their images expressed themselves.

This was a pattern I saw over and over as my cabinets became something of a community art project. For those who were creatively inhibited there was always **the protestation, the resignation, the quieting, and then the immersion.** It was funny to me that, despite the initial protestations, each person expressed a definite idea about what exactly would be drawn once they set themselves to the actual task. Watching this process, particularly the quieting when the creative connection was made, was truly beautiful. Nothing compares to seeing adults becoming as playful as children again. Every day I enter that room, I feel blessed with the memory of how each piece was created.

This hasn't been restricted to painted pictures. I've observed the same pattern in friends playing with magnetic poetry: **protestation, resistance, quieting, and immersion**. It isn't that what emerges is necessarily high art, and it isn't even important that anyone else understands it. Just hearing my Southside of Chicago, "regular guy" brother-in-law exclaim, "That's it! 'Tangy monkey!' That's perfect!" as he nods his head vigorously and links words together in a way none of us can fathom, is priceless. Seeing the connection and witnessing the joyful engagement with the creative process … watching someone play as they express something only they can bring forth (*"tangy monkey?!"*), is one of the most beautiful things I have ever seen (and, yes, sometimes the funniest). The memory makes me smile even as I write this.

You can observe a similar process if you watch room make-over shows. Invariably, they show a room that is bland and lifeless, a hodgepodge of objects with no sense of personality, rhythm or order. The couple explains that they simply didn't know what to do. Interestingly, once the transformation process has begun, hopes start to be expressed.

"I hope they use green. I love green." "I would love to see a tropical theme." "I'll hate it if it's too contemporary."

Reminds me of a saying I once heard, the source unknown: **"When we ask for advice, what we really want is permission."**

We've made creativity, including the process of creating *our own* home environment the purview of "qualified" professionals and "legitimate" artists. But watch the reactions closely during the home show "reveal." In that moment, you will see it.

*"This is just **what I had pictured**! It's what I had hoped!"* Or, *"This isn't at all what **I had in mind**!"*

It isn't about **becoming** creative. You already are. Yes, of course, you may need to learn a thing or two about the techniques and tools that will allow you the greatest expression of what you have inside, but all the technique in the world isn't going to make you creative. It will simply give you an outlet for its expression.

So, How Do You Get In Touch With Your Natural Creativity?

First, be realistic. If you have been out of touch with or actively denying your creativity for years, don't expect it to burst forth in full regalia just because you want it to now. *Why should it trust you?* If you have an over-active censor, perfectionist, or judge and jury living in your head, your heart may decide it simply isn't worth the risk to be held under that kind of scrutiny.

Yes. Your heart. Creativity isn't a head thing. Your head may try to argue this point. You may say, "I heard you have to pick complimentary colors on the color wheel." Or, "You need something black to ground a room." Or, "You shouldn't start a sentence with 'or'." Maybe.

But remember, there is a difference between creativity and creative technique. First, get it out. You can tweak it later.

Commit To Spending Time Alone. Regularly.

This is a tough one! The average American is highly over-stimulated and over-committed. Multitasking has become a way of life, as has caffeine consumption and an overflowing media diet. We are inundated with external messages from the minute the clock radio goes off in the morning, much of which is aimed, directly and deliberately, at your emotions. If you haven't heard, "emotional branding" is all the rage now. What this means for you is that a lot of people are getting paid a lot of money to figure out how to tap into and manipulate your emotions so that you will part with your money in exchange for whatever they want to sell you. If you don't believe me, just think back to the last time that a "great" sale hooked you in to buying something at a "low, low price you may never see again." And pay attention to the music they play in your favorite shops and restaurants and tell me they don't have your demographic pegged!

With your emotional life being a deliberate target for strategic marketing manipulation, how are you supposed to figure out how you really feel and what is really important to you? You aren't being asked to express yourself, authentically. You are being asked to buy in to the next trend; to reach for the next big thing. You aren't being asked to *be* the next big thing. If you really want to get in touch with your creativity, you have to be a strong and determined gate keeper defending your right to keep yourself clear of undue influences. Much easier said than done, but if practiced regularly, a little alone time can yield big results.

When I started working as a coach, I used to schedule morning sessions until I realized that once I started to focus on others I completely bypassed my connection to my own life. (This is a huge risk for all helping professionals.) By reserving my mornings for my own study, writing, and extended walks, I am able to open myself to the needs of my clients without sacrificing my connection to my own creativity and need for self-expression. I no longer run the risk of confusing my life with that of my clients. My creativity is nurtured and preserved and, as a result, I can be fully present to others when called to do so.

Be Willing To Stand Naked Before Yourself. Without Prejudice.

Here, I simply have to give it up to Clive Barker. Yes, Clive Barker of Hellraiser fame. A few months ago, as I was preparing to work on this chapter, I received a gift from a friend. It was Naomi Epel's *Writer's Dreaming*, which contains interviews of writers talking about how their dreams have influenced their creative process. I was delighted that the book should arrive at such an auspicious time in my own project. Doubly intriguing was the subject matter, as I have had a plethora of complex and intricate dreams that have fascinated and, at times, perplexed me with their richness.

Now, I admit I was going to skim, if not skip entirely, the chapter on Clive Barker. I confess that I have not read his works and have not seen any of the Hellraiser films, so I have no right to have an opinion on the man, but honestly, his name has never jumped out at me as one of the great authors of our time, as say a Maya Angelou or Isabelle Allende.

Imagine my surprise when I found myself absorbed in his chapter and highlighting line after line saying, "Yes, I understand this!" "I have thought this very thing myself!" "This is a marvelous insight!"

Consider these paragraphs on the interplay between waking and sleeping life and the process of allowing one's unconscious/subconscious life to be **acknowledged and given validity as an expression of some aspect of oneself and one's experience:**

"...*the idea of putting those things* [here he means dream images, some of which are quite disturbing] *into art is an important and interesting issue...simply to talk about them as things which have meaning, which are intimate self-confessions is, it seems to me, the primary act. The secondary act is the turning it into art...But to simply say I am whispering to myself through the lattice of my consciousness... and saying, I don't mind what I hear. I don't mind. I forbid myself nothing. I forbid my subconscious, and therefore my consciousness nothing, is the beginning, I think, of great health."*

Embracing Clive Barker-type dream images as an indication of great health?! I must say, this caught my attention. How many of us distance ourselves from our dreams (daydreams as well as night dreams), censoring ourselves very closely so that only "realistic," "rational," "beautiful," and otherwise acceptable thoughts gain our notice? How many of us hide our journals, or disturbing paintings, or simply refuse to commit uncensored work to concrete form for fear someone will find out about those parts of us we find shameful, disturbing, or unbecoming in some way?

This next paragraph refers to being completely open to oneself in the artistic process and echoes my sentiment that regular time alone is critical to evoking your Muse. Clive continues:

"This is an almost meditative activity, it seems to me. It's a question of sitting quietly with yourself and saying, the only company I have in all the world is the person I am. And everything else can go away from me, everybody else can go away from me. It is within the bounds of possibility that all the people I love most in the world could be gone tomorrow. I have to be at peace with this myself. And a third of this "myself" is a sleeping self. An important third, perhaps the most important third. So, let me be quiet with myself and sit with myself and like myself, and what my subconscious is telling me."

This is a **very** tall order for most of us. Even to acknowledge the fundamental fact that we are all we have in the end is way too real for most people to even come close to acknowledging. And making the commitment to like yourself, to embrace what you uncover in your own creative process and to be willing to learn from it…to be willing to open yourself to the purest expression of who you are, authentically…I have to agree with Clive, it is a sign of great health. Mr. Barker, you have blown my mind.

Be Curious About Your Creative Process and Expect Creative Results

There is a tremendous difference between being creative and simply being productive. For those of you who are used to multi-tasking, learning to release yourself into your natural creative rhythm can feel downright torturous. We have such an emphasis on personal productivity and speed to market for businesses in our culture that our internal processes very often are discounted, if not discouraged outright.

The reality is actual creative output is merely the tip of the iceberg that is the creative self. Each of us carries within ourselves a huge lab where great experiments are underway. Even as you read this, your internal alchemists are busily relating these words to other thoughts, insights, and experiences you have had and spinning them into your own unique perspective. Some of you reading this will be aware of this process and may even be making notes in the margins while you read. For others, this process may be happening largely outside your conscious awareness.

Whether you are aware of it or not, you are always taking in information from your environment and fitting it together in a way that tells the story of how you see the world and your place in it. Creativity is the process of turning that story into a dialogue within, whatever medium you choose. And, as we should do in any good conversation, sometimes we need to shut up and listen. And, sometimes, in really close relationships like best friends or old married couples in love, silence can be full and rich.

If you befriend your creative process and engage it in a conversation based on trust and respect, it will not disappoint you. Sometimes those internal alchemists simply need time to mull things over but, rest assured, they will mull them over. They can't help it. It's what they were built for. And they work without your conscious manipulation and control. That's the hard part for most of us; trusting that something is going on in there even when you aren't in control of it and don't see evidence of it on the outside. But if you have ever had a great thought in a dream, solved a problem while weeding your garden, or remembered that forgotten song title while you were in the shower, you have evidence that your mind will give up the goods once you relax a bit.

Once you trust yourself, you can actually program yourself to be ready when you need to be outwardly creative. I do this every time I have a project do. I look at the calendar, tell myself, "Okay, Brain, you have to be ready to write that chapter next Thursday. Start working on it. I'm going to go do laundry now." Because my creative self and I have an open and trusting relationship, this process has never failed me. I had to work up to trusting it with really big projects, but it has passed every test.

Pavlov's Dog... What Every Pet Knows

If you are a pet owner, you are aware of the uncanny way your cat seems to know when you are about to open the can of cat food, or the way your dog knows when you are getting the leash for a walk. Pavlov's dog knew that the sound of the bell meant food was on its way and would begin salivating just at the sound. In psychology, this is called classical conditioning and, I hate to break it to you, but you and Pavlov's dog have a lot in common. The good news is, now you have a wonderful opportunity to train yourself to be creative when you want to be!

You may have heard that some artists and athletes have rituals they employ when they are being called upon to perform. This is the same principle with which we are working. Our environment and our rituals become associated with the activity we are engaging in. I was accidentally conditioned in childhood when we did our Sunday house cleaning while my dad played his stereo. To this day, whenever I hear Marvin Gaye's "What's Goin' On?" I get a nearly uncontrollable urge to clean the kitchen. In fact, when I need to clean and am not in the mood, I put Marvin on the stereo and instantly I become the White Tornado.

You can do exactly the same thing. Create the environment that most supports your creativity and **set it up consistently**. Consistency is the key here. Your brain will then associate the environment with the activity. When I write my coaching newsletter, I always begin with my cup of tea and burning incense while at the computer. In fact, I have incense going right now. This sends the signal to my brain, "Oh, it must be time for some focused writing now," and the process begins to flow almost effortlessly as a result.

Speaking of Cleaning...
Move Your Body, Use Your Hands!

I can't emphasize this enough. Just as I said earlier that you are always taking in information from your environment that can be used as creative grist for the mill, it's important to realize that your entire body is taking in information. You are taking in smells, sounds, physical sensations, tastes, just as you are taking in visual input and information. Creative processing takes place on a whole body level. Watch people's hands while they talk if

↓ focusing tools

you don't believe me. Even if your creative mode of expression does not involve your entire body, your creative **processing** will be enhanced by the use of your body. Simple, repetitive tasks, like weeding the garden, ironing, walking, riding your bike, and washing dishes can be wonderful focusing tools. Cleaning closets is nearly a silver bullet for removing creative blocks. Don't be deceived. These activities are not procrastination when you have developed the relationship with your creative self that allows you to trust that internal processing is going on. You just have to keep your promise to show up and give it an outlet later. Don't forget that those rituals to coax it out will help that process considerably!

↖ show up

Creative Risks/Creative Gambles

If you are new to exploring your creativity, make sure you don't scare yourself silly by taking on something too big or too public. It's okay, and sometimes very wise, to let your first creative efforts stay under the radar of family, friends, and talent scouts. Accept that you will have a technical learning curve as you master the medium you adopt and that this learning process will result in a deepening of your understanding of your own creative voice (or artistic eye). Your understanding will lead you to learn more specific technical aspects of your work and this, in turn, will enrich your voice. This conversation between you, yourself, and your medium will be plenty at first. Later, you can pick the most comfortable of the uncomfortable options for making your efforts more public. Put one or two eggs in your psychic basket and let the feedback develop you. Resist the temptation to base your ultimate worth as a creative being on what you produce and share when you are still learning. And you will always be learning. You may always need a day job to support your creative endeavors. Don't let that derail you or force you to devalue your creative process. The process is the thing…let yourself enter the dialogue without demands on the outcome. Creativity is a process through which you will discover yourself. This will be a lot easier when you are willing to believe you are someone worth getting to know.

Finally, a Word About Critics
(From Within and Without)

Don't confuse the significance of your creative voice with the quality of your creative technique. Work on technical growth, but while you are on your way to mastery keep a look out for your artistic perspective. Technique can always be developed and your artistic stirrings will tell you where technique needs developing for its most potent expression.

When you show your work to others, don't be surprised if most people assume you want a response to the technical merit of your creation. And, of course, you do. But be sure to take an expanded vision of your work and don't let technical critics put spells on you that silence your artistic voice. If someone launches in to a technical evaluation of your work without bothering to express curiosity about what you were trying to say or what attracted you to the subject or the medium you chose, the value of the critique is compromised. If the intended message is understood, it is much easier to assess where and why the work did or didn't live up to what you have envisioned. With that level of understanding, and with your ego out of the way for the sake of your development, your skills can be grown and developed. Critique without context is dangerous. Critique born out of understanding and a true desire to communicate something that is important to you to share is priceless and can be transformative for a creative person. Comparing your technical expertise to the student next to you in art class, or to your best friend, or Picasso simply compares tool kit to tool kit. Let it inspire you and motivate you but never let that stop you from being curious about your unique creative perspective. Allow yourself to imitate styles, try different approaches, and willingly immerse yourself in the process of allowing your perspective its truest expression.

Let yourself surprise yourself.

Now go play; your aliens await…

About
Laura Young

Wellness Coach, Laura Young, M.A., founded Wellspring Coaching in 1999. Her innovative approach to wellness draws upon 25 years of experience, including extensive background in the fields of psychology, pain management, personal development coaching, martial arts, meditation, and yoga. She is a dedicated student of both Eastern and Western philosophy. Her interest in the field of creativity has been fueled by her repeated professional observation of the transformative power of story and the power of creative expression to promote wellness.

Having worked extensively with both healthy and chronically ill adults, Laura has had a unique opportunity to study the nature of wellness holistically and has gained an understanding of why many self help models ultimately fail those who attempt to use them. Traditionally, self-help and stress management techniques focus on ways to improve self-care. We may journal in private, post affirmations on our mirrors, and light scented candles, but often these techniques do not translate into how a person is to live day to day in relation to the complex demands of home and career. The techniques often become little more than bandages and temporary escapes from larger life problems.

Clearly, effective wellness models need to move beyond the mere promotion of self-soothing and self-understanding. Being able to stand outside oneself to gain understanding of one's life challenges and reactions to them is a critical piece of living a healthy, balanced life, but is not sufficient.

Wellness creates a sense of connection and meaning in life. We are all part of a larger world. You may have a family, friends, co-workers, a church, or other community. Beyond our human connections, we also have connections with nature, and many have a sense of spiritual connection to something greater than oneself.

Wellness is mind-body-spirit *integration* that promotes self-care and self-understanding *and* connects one's life to the larger world. It is a state of being joyfully and enthusiastically engaged with one's life, even when it doesn't turn out exactly as one had planned.

If you have been struggling with keeping your sense of center in the midst of life pressures, or have an interest in deepening your own understanding and practical application of wellness principles to promote an ongoing sense of joyful engagement with your life, please feel invited to contact Laura. Her website, www.wellspringcoaching.com links to extensive writings on a number of personal development topics, including those highly relevant to mid-lifers. If you wish to schedule a private consultation, she may be reached at Laura@wellspringcoaching.com or by calling 630-562-1877.

Becoming a Butterfly:
Living Your Creative Expression

By Gwen Thelen

Have you ever driven by a big green, grassy hill at a public park and felt the urge to get out of your car, climb to the top, and roll all the way down? Or, you hear a song piped in at the grocery store and feel like dancing to it for a moment? Maybe you've walked by a display of art supplies and had the urge to buy some? Have you ever been riding your bike along a bike path, and burst out in song? Or maybe you desire to start your own business, dig out all the grass in your front yard and plant it full of wildflowers, build furniture, or live in the wilderness. These urges are life, longing to be creatively expressed through you.

Though creativity is often associated with the arts, it is not limited to that. I believe that creativity is the making and expression of life. We consciously engage in creative endeavors because they give meaning and form to our lives and who we are. Acts of creation are fun, intensify life, give emotional release, have transformational power, lead us to greater awareness, understanding, and insight into ourselves, and give our lives meaning and intention. Creative expression is the natural result of following an urge, a drive that is within each of us. And acting on our urges to create informs the direction of our lives.

I believe that the sheer act of creative expression is our birthright. We are all Creatives. Here, I deliberately use creative as a noun. You automatically are creative. It is not something you earn, it is not a special gift you get, it's not even something you can develop! It just *is*. I believe all children know this until it is trained out of them. I was no exception. Into my young adulthood, people would see my art and say, "Oh! You're an artist!" I would shrug and say, "Well, not really," believing I didn't qualify.

From the moment we're born, we're creatively expressing ourselves. My two children are living proof of this. They simply follow what compels them. They have danced in the grocery store plenty of times. I've ridden behind them while they're belting out a tune from Aladdin on their bikes, lain out countless pencils, crayons, and paper on a daily basis, and yes, I've stretched out on the grass numerous times at their encouragement to race them down the hill, though I can never seem to win because my roll always goes sideways.

Wrapping Up in a Protective Cocoon

By adolescence many of us begin to pull ourselves inward, eventually wrapping ourselves in a protective cocoon that becomes so cozy, we are lulled to sleep. Somewhere along the line, we stop trusting our desire to create. We stop following what compels us, our mouths stop singing, bodies stop dancing, imagination is dulled. For some, this creative expression remains hidden away into adulthood, never to emerge into its full butterfly-like expression again. We think that by pulling inward, we'll protect ourselves from risk, ridicule, invalidation, scoff, or failure. Ultimately, we become an adult whose creative expression is blocked by fear. We become so blocked that we may not even *feel* the desire to actively and consciously create. And we wonder why we're as busy as we have ever been, but we still feel like something's missing.

When does our creative expression get stifled? When do we decide it's not okay to roll down the hill, to move our bodies when we feel compelled to dance or to sing a little song out loud in a public place? When did we stop trusting ourselves and start saying things like, "I can't draw. I'm not pretty enough. Acting just isn't for me. I can't do *that*. What? Me? *Create* that? *Do* that? *Be* that?"?

I believe this hiding of our creative expression doesn't have to happen. But, because it has for so many of us, how can we reawaken our own metamorphosis and reclaim the natural *urge* to create? How can we see that breaking out of this cocoon will free us to be the colorful butterfly we were meant to be; one that flies with freedom in any direction that we desire?

I grew up in a large family of thirteen on a 60-acre farm in the middle of Minnesota, with no television. What a playground! The setting was ripe with opportunities to be creative in every way I could imagine. I was fortunate to have had a father and mother who believed that the joy for children is in their freedom to be creative. My siblings and I played in the summer months for hours out in the cornfields and wooded groves where our houses were built of air and branches, clouds and dirt. We ran the length of our farmyard hundreds of times a day, beating our little naked feet against the ground, laughing the whole way. In the winter months, we took to our art supplies. We had differing degrees of talent, but no lack of desire. Some of us drew corn stalks, animals, airplanes, and people's noses, while others preferred to color within the lines of Pinocchio's hat. Grouped around the table with my brothers and sisters, I heard the sound of pencils scratching against paper, the *woooochhh* of the scissors splitting a piece of cardboard into two, and the scritch-scratch of the eraser correcting a line gone astray.

I remember creating with abandon at an old kitchen table that creaked with every lean from having born the weight of 26 elbows each evening for dinner. We were generous with our compliments to one another despite the intense, inevitable competition between us. My siblings I and were both admired and envied by one another, as well as admiring and envious. Self-esteem soared when my artistic expression was supported, appreciated, understood, and valued by those who had the greatest influence in my young life at the time: my family. The talent to draw well was valued in my family; it was considered my special God-given talent.

At the time, my young understanding of an "artist" was that of a person who had talent, training, and a gift for the creative. So it was no surprise to me when my older sister announced that she was headed off to school to be*come* an artist. I had come to understand that an artist wasn't, in fact, something that you automatically *were,* but something that you must go to school to be*come.* I deduced at a very young age that because I did not come up with great, original ideas *and* I didn't have the training, I was clearly *not* an artist, but rather, was simply "good at drawing."

So I went with my understanding that I simply had a talent to draw well. As a child I felt confident when art time would roll around. It was in those moments that I shined the brightest. Trust in my peers, teachers, and myself grew as appreciation for my work was expressed. I was merely compelled to draw; I listened and acted on that desire.

Making Compromising Trades

As happens to most of us starting when we're young, we begin to make small trades along the way with our life experiences because of little lies that we believe. We trade in faith for disbelief, trust for doubt, freedom for prison. These trades result in forming negative core beliefs about who we are and what we are (or are not) capable of. These negative beliefs always come with a price. They block our creativity and keep us from manifesting our highest potential. These beliefs are critical to our development as Creatives—and go far in determining the distance to which we will go, the height to which we will fly.

I was in the first grade. After playing outside, the chattering class had all settled into their small desks anticipating art time. For our project, we were all to make a single flower with three leaves, laid down on a piece of green construction paper. The unique part about this art assignment was that the leaves were to be made of fabric. I observed how beautifully my teacher had completed her flower as an example for the class to follow. I was excited about creating mine to look exactly like hers, all crisp and perfect. After cutting out the stem and flower petals, I carefully glued them onto the papery bed of grass. With anticipation, I clasped my fingers around the fabric, which would soon be transformed from a simple square to beautiful, realistic leaves. I pinched the scissors down over the material. Disappointed, I noticed that the fabric jaggedly resisted my efforts to cut a smooth, sharp line. "What is wrong with my scissors?" I wondered.

Glancing around the room, not wanting to draw attention to myself, I continued to struggle. Stealing glimpses at the other children, I noticed how effortlessly they were completing their magnificent pictures with perfectly cut leaves placed neatly on their stems. Feeling self conscious, I began to think that I was not as good as the others. I felt my face get hot as I lost the nerve to ask the teacher for help. In my mind at that moment, I was the *only* one who couldn't cut the fabric well. Hot tears welled up in my eyes as I continued to struggle.

A large hand roughly snatching the scissors from mine met my frustration. My teacher impatiently mumbled under her breath and with several rushed slices, produced two nasty looking leaves that randomly fell to my desk. As she finished, she let the scissors fall to the desk and marched away. Embarrassed and deflated, the joy in my art-making drained out of me. Strongly reinforced by the teacher, I felt sure that something was wrong with me. In that instant, I traded faith in my abilities and myself for a negative core belief that was to follow me for years afterward: "I am stupid." My first trade.

As an adolescent, I participated in many singing groups for my high school. I had numerous opportunities to perform solos and duets at various school performances. Though I could hold a tune, singing was not something in which I had confidence. Though it was enjoyable, it still required a tremendous amount of courage to sing in front of others. I remember always feeling terribly nervous, afraid and unsure of myself before a performance. I recall one music teacher who was very passionate about music. I believed he knew more than anyone about music and thus granted him the power to tell me what was good and what wasn't. After one such performance where I sang a duet with a fellow student, I asked him for some feedback. Eagerly anticipating a constructive reply, I was met with his head held high and eyes slightly averted. He replied with a smirk, "You were pretty good, but a little off key." In that moment, I made another trade; freedom for another imprisoning belief: "I am not good enough."

Without even realizing it, I gave the power over to someone else to decide who I was, how good I was, or even *if* I was good at all! Unknowingly, I began to take on negative core beliefs based on another's perspective. Beliefs like: "I'm not good enough," or

"They will laugh at me if I act out of the ordinary" and "I am just not smart enough." Like many others, at such an early age, I was not taught that another's perspective, whether true or not, is simply that—*their* perspective, one that is a reflection of their experience and has nothing to do with mine.

Material For the Cocoon

From the moment we are born, we are immersed in a culture that gives us messages like, "Artist's starve," "Follow the well-trodden path, and for goodness sakes, *don't* reinvent the wheel," and "Life happens *to* you." We mistakenly wrap ourselves in these messages. We take them as truth and unknowingly thwart our own process. After all, everyone else believes these messages, so they must be true!

I imagine those who thought the world was flat looked out at the horizon and made the choice *not* to travel toward it for fear they would fall off the other side! It's the same way with the powerful messages we're given. Those messages are not based in love, but in fear. Each of us has our own unique set of messages that we took on as part of our belief system. These messages, combined with one's trades, provide an illusionary safety from risk, ridicule, exclusion, success, failure; whatever the person is afraid of losing...or gaining!

In my twenties, I conducted my life very carefully. For years I avoided experiences that might result in my looking stupid or had a high risk of mistakes. Though I continued to create art sporadically, I sometimes did not do any art for a year or more at a time.

At one point, I excitedly discovered that I was particularly talented at painting portraits. I was driven to paint those portraits, and nothing could stop me from listening to that voice. I experienced a great deal of joy while painting those whom I loved and gave much of my art away as gifts. These were always received well.

Urged by my friends and family, I decided to start my own portraiture business and enthusiastically launched into my work. On several occasions during the first few months, I received feedback that I had made several mistakes in my clients' portraits. This type of response about my work made me feel intensely uncomfortable and all I knew was that I did not want to experience it. Within months, I began to make excuses for why I had not been drawing portraits, "I've got so much *other* work to do" or "I don't really enjoy doing this kind of art anyway." It did not take much for me to determine that I must not be cut out to be a portrait artist. I was spending so much time and energy designing a story around why I *couldn't* that I was blinded to the fact that I *could.* I started saying things like, "People are simply too demanding, unrealistic, and have set their expectations too high!"

Though I did not recognize it at the time, this perceived negative feedback touched on the beliefs I already had about myself that I was not smart or talented enough and mistake prone. So, I chose to quit out of fear that "they" might be right. I thought that by quitting, I could avoid feeling stupid and making mistakes. I thought that the more I turned away from my desire to create, the less I would risk rejection.

Facing Freedom

What I didn't understand at the time was that going toward and through my fears would result in my own freedom from a prison to which only I had the key! To be free is our true nature and creativity is freedom!

Finding true nature is not for the faint at heart. It requires courage, a sense of adventure, and a fearless heart. A fearless heart is not one that does not have fear; but it is rather a heart that knows what to do in the face of it. When you understand that your fears are a beacon to your truth, you'll have the courage to walk through them. I remember being told once by a brave soul, "Sometimes you've just got to go out and scare yourself!" Sometimes you've just got to face what scares you the most. When you do this, you'll find that what shows up on the other side are all those truths that you traded in long ago for negative core beliefs. Beliefs are exactly that—*beliefs*, not facts. This is why, when facing your fears you will experience these negative beliefs fall away. They are simultaneously replaced by the truth of who you really are—which is a dynamic, creative, and powerful individual, capable of creation itself.

Choosing to Become the Butterfly

The results come down to choices, and everyone has them. We have a choice to awaken to our creativity or not. When we choose not to create out of fear of what may come, our lives become flat, unfulfilling, and just plain mind numbing. Imagine sleeping in a cocoon for the duration of your life, afraid of what might happen if you emerge!

Indeed, we are creating our lives the entire time, sleeping or awake, aware of it or not. The disadvantage to creating while sleeping is that we allow our fears, doubts, and negative core beliefs to run us, influencing every decision we make. It is these fears that block us from living our best lives as creative beings. Not only did these blocks negatively influence my artistic expression, but the way I expressed myself in *every*thing, from the way I dressed to the way I expressed myself within my relationships. For me, fear ruled and resulted in my choice to discontinue painting portraits. I chose to live in fear, put my pencils and paints away, and curled up for a nice long nap.

But here is where it gets interesting. You see, despite fear, creativity can't help itself! It's a part of us whether we're aware of it or not. And though it may appear that the worm is doing nothing in its cocoon, it is waiting for nature's nudge to wake up into something else: a butterfly! We all get this nudge sooner or later. The question is, is the nudge hard enough to rouse us from our fearful slumber?

Many of us have lives that are so packed with activities that it is difficult to feel this nudge, or hear our lives calling for us. Sometimes this shows up as the feeling that there is something missing in our lives. Somehow, we're not quite fulfilled or satisfied. There seems to be something gently shaking our shoulder, but we just can't open our eyes wide enough to see what it is.

I was certainly no exception. The unsettled feeling of something missing bubbled up years later and I began to listen and then pose the questions, "Where is my passion? Where is my laughter? Where is my desire to create? Why does life feel so flat?" It wasn't until I went back to college and entered my final semester that the answers began to come.

That spring was filled with classes in art, dance, writing, and voice. It was also one of the most intensely difficult, terrifying, and revealing times of my life. Through artistic, creative expression, I truly began to wake up to what was missing in my life: the feeling of freedom to express my authentic self in my own unique way, as well as the full acceptance of that expression. Breaking through my fear and resistance while my judge and inner critic shouted from the gallery of voices behind me, bombarding me with my habitual cruelty, reminding me of all my powerful negative core beliefs took courage. "You'll make a fool of yourself!" "They'll hate you!" "They'll reject you!" "You'll look stupid and clumsy!" "What are you thinking?"

As I witnessed other students step up and reveal themselves through their artistic medium, I began to see how each of them had a beautifully unique and authentic way of expressing him or herself. I soon began to recognize and appreciate the beauty in my own unique expression, not only in my artistic endeavors, but also in the way I spoke, dressed, walked, laughed, and how I expressed myself within my own relationships.

Literally, I was able to stand face-to-face with my fears of self-expression. I met my creative edge by having to put paint on the canvas, sing out loud, and dance. Creative expression had become a metaphor for my life, a window to my soul, a tool for growth in that it was a clear reflection of the way I approached, created, and feared my own life. By taking risks and pushing my edge creatively in art, voice, sound, and movement, I found that I started to become more willing to do the same in my life.

Within my experience of freedom, I simultaneously felt a falling away of the pressure to get it right, the fear of criticism or failure, and the worry about what others would think. I awakened and fully embraced my own unique expression that only I could bring to the world.

For me, it was artistic expression that served to shine a light on my fears, doubts, blocks, and resistance. With that light on I was able to see how I was living, fearing, and unconsciously creating my life. Through it, I awoke to and experienced the value of my own creative expression and was able to reclaim my power to both change and consciously create my life. The prison was unlocked, the cocoon broke open, and I stepped through the opening into my power to express a life of freedom and to boldly show the colors of my new wings! I had rediscovered my true nature!

Are You Ready to Set Yourself Free?

The question is, are you awake to your true creative nature or are you sleeping? Are you bound in your own fearful wrapping or free?

Wake up and free yourself from your own cocoon of fear. Embrace and accept the creative part of you that longs for expression and then celebrate it by taking action! Go ahead and dance when you hear your favorite song—wherever you are. Roll down a grassy hill, buy those art supplies, and burst out in song while riding your bike. Go ahead and start that business you've always dreamed of, go camping for a month in Alaska, or build that stone path in your back yard! Take that chance and follow what compels you. I assure you, when you listen to and follow your desires, your life will joyfully inform you and make clear the direction of your life. Everyone is entitled to the joy that is found in free creative expression!

When you listen, when you wake up, when you follow your heart, when you face your fears, when you choose your creativity— you will find your truth.

And here I find myself writing, when I never considered myself a writer, painting portraits in ways that are continually surprising, raising my two children with laughter, working with people in ways that inspire, move, and nourish me. I wake up each day, with eyes open wide, curiously anticipating what surprises my day might bring. I have become the butterfly; I am living my creative expression.

About
Gwen Thelen

"What do you know for sure?" A question that usually brought a long-winded response from me is now quickly answered: "If we can accept the fact that we are not separate from one another but rather deeply connected, then we are capable of experiencing our innate nature, which is the state of *being in* Love."

I've always considered myself a seeker. My closest friends will tell you that I continually ask questions primarily aimed at discovering more about the human body, mind, and spirit. Having spent eight years coaching and training groups and individuals about physical wellness, I found myself asking more and more questions about the mind and spirit. These questions led me to study Contemplative Psychology and Expressive Arts in Healing at Naropa University and seek certification as a Life Coach through the International Coach Academy. They also led me through the death of my mother, my divorce, and my fierce grappling with the search for my authentic self. During this period I'd been greatly influenced by Deepak Chopra's writings about the power of the mind and the truth of the spirit that lives within us.

Ultimately, we are one with all of life. It is this very truth that strongly motivates and continues to inform my way of being as a woman, mother, daughter, sister, lover, and friend. I cannot think of a better way to live my life except through the knowing that my life purpose is fully served when I choose Love.

For more information, visit www.wideawakecoaching or www.therevolutionislove.com, call 303-818-0532, or email gwenthelen@msn.com.

How Many Colors Are There In Your Rainbow? An Invitation to Experience Diversity

By Aline Vieira

Have you ever played with your computer screen's resolution? Try it! Go to your computer monitor settings and you will see a little rainbow of colors: red, orange, yellow, green, blue, indigo, violet, and many in between. Try experimenting by changing the number of pixels. As you increase the pixel count, you add more colors to that little rainbow, increasing your screen resolution, which gives you a clearer image.

What would it be like to have the same opportunity to experiment with the image of the world around you? You have the opportunity right now. I am inviting you to look at a few ways you can change the settings in your consciousness so that your view of the world will become clearer and your outlook in life will gain more precision. You can accomplish that by experimenting with diversity.

You live in a world surrounded by many kinds of diversity: cultural, spiritual, racial, life style, political, and many more. Experiencing diversity of any kind allows you to rethink, reframe, and raise your current paradigm to a higher level. As you move through these experiences, you learn to detach from values and beliefs that are relative *only* to your current circumstances. You can then replace these temporary values and beliefs with everlasting, *absolute ones*, which will be the foundation for the life that your heart truly desires. Every time you go through this process, a new color is added to the rainbow of your consciousness. With each new color, you become more aware—an increase of consciousness—and the world around you gains more precision and meaning.

The result of increased consciousness is the ability to create the life you want instead of following "fate" and living reactively.

This newfound level of consciousness allows you to go from a place of being a "survivor" and getting by with every day life to a place of being the "creator" of your own destiny. And that is what Creative Intelligence is: the **power to create**.

Several major life lessons came to me through experiencing **cultural** diversity. Although they were seemingly minor experiences, they resulted in tremendous, life-changing breakthroughs, allowing my consciousness to flourish. As a result, my ability to make better choices and decisions for my life has increased tremendously. I have learned how to be the creator of my life.

In this chapter, I would like to share some of these paradigm shifts with you, with the hope that my experience will inspire you to bring your own consciousness to the next level and access more of your own Creative Intelligence. I will also ask you to journal on these ideas as steps to your own self-evaluation.

Black: Emptiness – The Absence of Consciousness

When I first took a look at my life at a very young age, I saw a rainbow with no colors, just black. I wondered how much more there was to life. I was then a 12-year old introvert, with no courage to reach out to touch life. I was in 7th grade, living in my home country of Brazil. Then, one day, a simple reading assignment changed everything. The book we were given to read was *Jonathan Livingston Seagull*, by Richard Bach. The story is about a bird who has a tremendous desire to challenge his limits and grow to the next level. As I read that book, I realized for the first time that there was a next level, and that I had the option to go there. What an exciting moment! A vision flashed right in front of me. I could feel it! I could taste it! I could smell it! I wanted to fly and just *be*!

I had just seen a huge vision unfolding right before my eyes, but I did not know how to make it a part of my life. For a long time, I just kept it to myself. I concealed it, stuffed it away, and went on living the next several years of my life with my old black rainbow, waiting for a miracle to happen and the right winds to blow so that I could take off on that flight, just like Jonathan.

I continued to live my life following social expectations as a domesticated bird in my assigned cage. My culture expected me to put all my energy toward becoming that perfect girl and prepare for my prince who would come on a white horse, marry me, and we would live happily ever after. I prepared myself for that prince, and waited for him as my youth went by. I was tremendously unhappy putting all my energy into being who I "should" have been, instead of who I really wanted to be. I behaved like that perfect individual on the outside, but deep inside I felt as far as possible from being that person. Deep inside I wanted to fly away, fly high, dream, live out my vision, and just be *me*.

I started to question and God started to answer. I learned about opportunities in the United States. That was the place to be, a place where dreams come true, a land of milk and honey. I started to wonder how my life might be in that country I had always heard so many great things about. Suddenly a huge sense came over me that the time to fly away had arrived. At age 24, I opened my cage door and came to the United States of America. Looking back, I realize the real reason why I came to the U.S. was not because it was the best place to be, nor because I picked it. I came to the U.S. because God brought me here. I realize that this country was the place He picked for me to learn my life lessons. It was the perfect schoolroom for me to experience diversity and learn the power to create. My journey to consciousness began.

Journaling for consciousness: How are you living your life right now? Are you being that person you want to be or are you living day-by-day following social expectations? How would you like to fly to the next level?

Red: Beliefs – Reframing Your Thinking

I arrived in the U.S. with $300 in my pocket, a below average knowledge of English, and a huge desire in my heart to grow and become my best. I was prepared to work hard and make my way to the top. With much commitment and the support of God-sent mentors, I was able to overcome all the great expected challenges: getting around town, finding my way through campus, learning to deal with weather changes, figuring out the right clothes to wear for the season, and even walking on ice without breaking a leg. At that point, I felt all I needed was to get a job and I would be all "set."

I started to look for work around campus, but I could not find anything at "my level." I had just come from Brazil, where I had left a nice job in a beautiful office in the rich part of my city, and had the hopes of finding a comparable job on campus. After all, I was already a professional with some work experience under my belt. However, much to my surprise, there were no office jobs available. The only job I was able to find was in the cafeteria preparing the salad bar. I was devastated. "Work in a cafeteria?" I asked myself. "I don't think so!" In my culture, that job was considered a "low class" job. "What would my friends back home say?"

After contemplating the issue, I realized that this was the only job available to me, and with much reluctance, I took it. On my first day at work, with heaviness in my heart, I put on my blue polyester apron, wiped back my tears, and proceeded to prepare that salad bar. I cut the vegetables and put them all in their respective containers, then went to set up the bar. That was all okay. I just had one major concern: I did not want any of my new friends to see me doing that "low class" work.

Sweating in fear of being caught by my new acquaintances, I kept my head down, as I did not want anyone to recognize me. Nearly at the end of the lunch hour, I thought I had made it through my first day without being caught. I could not wait to leave work and get back into my normal life. At five minutes to closing, I saw a girl I had just met coming toward me. I could not let her see me! But with no place to hide, I had to just face her. She walked up to me and, with a big smile, she said, "Hi. Do you work here?"

"Yes, I do," I replied with embarrassment. She smiled even bigger and, with great pride, she said, "What a coincidence! I do too." She obviously had no worries about what I was going to think or say. A huge weight lifted from my shoulders and a great sense of freedom filled my soul. I had just been freed from a huge stereotype. I understood that, in America, it was okay for a student to hold that type of job. I realized that my fear of being caught was simply the result of old beliefs.

With that breakthrough, I learned that the concept of different working classes was not as important as I thought it was. In fact, it was not important at all. Dispensing with that belief freed me to enjoy that job and to explore and experience other jobs on campus, regardless of what type of work it was. That freedom allowed me to *create* the financial support I needed to continue my education in America. That freedom came from my paradigm shift. ***The color red was added to my rainbow.***

Journaling for consciousness: How do beliefs control your life? Make a list of some of your current beliefs that have negatively influenced you. Choose one specific belief. How can you reframe it in such a way that it will increase your creative power?

Orange: Interpretation – Creating a New Meaning

Halfway through my freshmen year, I was still fairly new to America. At that point along my journey, I was not yet able to relate much to the American students. There were still some cultural differences I was not yet ready to embrace. But that was okay! I did not relate to them, and they did not relate to me. No problem! I made the decision to focus on becoming friends with the other international students on campus.

I became especially close with some folks from the other Latin American countries—Mexico, Costa Rica, Venezuela, Colombia—and started to learn some Spanish expressions. We would often get together, sit around, and laugh over the differences between the meanings of words from one country to another, and from one culture to another. For example, in my native Portuguese, the word *"embaraçada"* means, "embarrassed." In Spanish, however, it means "pregnant." They sounded like the same words, but they had totally different meanings. Differences such as this one resulted in little more than humor. However, there were also some of those awkward instances where cultural interpretation caused hurt feelings and division among us. These instances became yet another great lesson, an enormous concept.

I learned that words have as much weight as I believe they do. I learned that many times I can become offended simply because I interpret the meaning of certain words, statements, or expressions differently than how they may be intended. I create my interpretations based on my own internal culture. I have my own inner filters through which I perceive the world, and I only let in what matches what is already there. Meanwhile, when others express themselves, they are talking from their heart, from their own perception of the world around them. This lesson taught me that I have the power to reframe the meaning of what I hear before allowing it to settle in my consciousness. This new concept empowered me to stop negative energy from controlling my life, and allowed positive, creative energy to replace it. I was offered a new lesson and I embraced it. *The color orange was added to my rainbow.*

Journaling for consciousness: Have you ever found yourself caught up in someone's statement and struggling with what he or she might have meant? Think of a time when someone's statement might have produced a negative impact in you. How can you interpret that statement, giving it a new meaning so that you will feel positive about it?

Yellow: Assumption – Shifting Your Perspective

While still in college, I also became friends with some students from Southeast Asia—India, Sri-Lanka, Pakistan, Bangladesh. I would go to their dinner parties, sit around, and compare cultures, one of my favorite pastimes. Even though we were from opposite sides of the world and anyone would agree that we were completely different, I realized the opposite. We were actually incredibly alike. We just had different ways of accomplishing the same things. These students became like family to me. Getting to know them exposed me to some of the best cuisine from around the world. What an art to learn to mix the spices the way they did . . . coriander, turmeric, curry. I learned to cook the Southeast Asian food . . . curry chicken, papadum, dal, tandoori. I learned to appreciate it. I learned to eat it . . . *with my hands,* just as they did. That experience was exceptionally shocking to me, and yet so exotic and inspiring. As I learned to embrace such a new concept, enormous freedom filled my spirit.

I learned that in different parts of the world, there are completely different etiquette rules. I learned that the manners I worked so hard to learn were not the only way. There was at least one more way. And if there is one more way, there must be many other ways. This lesson taught me that I was free to create my own set of table etiquette . . . life etiquette . . . life values. Eating with these friends became a spiritual experience, a communion, a celebration of the world of diversity. A shift in my consciousness expanded my paradigm. *The color yellow was added to my rainbow.*

Journaling for consciousness: Do you ever find yourself committed to a restricted set of rules in any area of your life? Describe one specific rule that controls your life meaninglessly. What assumptions are keeping that rule as part of your current values system? How can you create freedom in your life by eliminating those assumptions from your guiding principles?

Green: Connection – Deepening Relationships

Of the many great international friends I made on campus, there was a very special one: a girl from Japan. She was an awesome and caring friend, but there was one thing in our interactions that I could not understand. She would never look me in the eyes. Her ways intrigued me until I learned that in her culture it was rude, even considered confrontational, to look someone in the eyes. Therefore, because she had respect for me, she would not look me straight in the eyes. I, on the other hand, had learned all my life that looking at others in the eyes means that I am honest, a person of integrity. I was raised to look into a person's eyes so that he or she would know that I was telling the truth. But she was told the exact opposite. Which way is the right way? Because we treasured our friendship, we were able to look past that, talk about this difference, and even laugh at it together. Breaking through this barrier allowed us to meet at a deeper level, connecting heart-to-heart.

How many times have we bought into "the right way" to express how we feel and who we are? How many times have we been told, "Don't say it that way, you will give the wrong impression," or, "Don't cross your legs or your arms, that shows resistance," or, "That is not the right thing to do; where did you learn that?" From this experience, I learned that the right thing for me to do is that one thing that feels right for me. And, in turn, I learned that the right thing for others is what feels right for them. This experience helped me be more able to accept others for who they are, as well as accept myself for who I am. Now I have a new paradigm. *A new color was added to my rainbow, and this time the color was green.*

Journaling for consciousness: How do you feel when others have entirely different manners than yours? Does that stop you from connecting with them? How can you bypass all that and create a connection straight from your soul to their soul?

Blue: Acceptance – Embracing Others

My college life was rich. I met many amazing folks from around the world. I learned their culture, I danced their dance, I wore their clothes, and I ate their food. But, it all came to an end when I graduated and got my first job. At that point, I thought the cross-cultural lessons I had learned in school were it. My life was going to be much easier, just gliding on the wind. After all, I had a degree, a job with a corresponding paycheck, and my first car. I had made it! Little did I know, I was about to face the greatest challenge of all: discrimination.

I had left the sheltered school environment where I was the exotic Brazilian student, and found myself in the American corporate world, an environment were I was the "stranger." The winds started to blow stronger, and my journey to higher consciousness became tougher. I did not have my international friends around me, and cultural differences were not fun anymore—just frustrating. I did not understand the people around me, and they did not understand me. I was not part of their cliques, was not included in their discussions, and was not invited to their parties. I was alone.

They were isolating me, ignoring me, discriminating against me. So, I built a whole set of explanations as to why they were treating me that way: "They don't know better." "They think I am strange because they have never been to a different country." "*They* believe . . . ." "*They* are assuming . . . ." "*They*. . . ."

That thinking pattern went on for a while, until a Greek friend of mine asked me, "Have you thought that you may be the one discriminating against them? Yes, they don't accept you for who you are. But do you accept them for who they are? Can you accept them not accepting you?" I had not thought of that! Could I accept the fact that it is okay for someone to not accept me?

With that, I learned that I was the one who was being judgmental. I learned that every time I face discrimination, I might be the one creating the discrimination. With that, I learned that once I accepted them, in turn, they would accept me. Acceptance is a two-way street. To this day, I have become very close friends with many Americans, and I have learned to embrace the American culture and make it part of my own personal culture. *The color blue was added to the rainbow of my consciousness.*

Journaling for consciousness: Think of a group among which you feel discriminated against. What do you think about them? How possible is it for your thinking to be the culprit to creating that energy? How can you change your thinking so that you can feel accepted in those relationships?

Indigo: Expression – Being Your True Self

With all those lessons under my belt, and somewhat adapted to American Corporate, I was ready to go to the next level. Now it was time for me to fly higher, to take the risk to express myself to the American world. I decided to develop my speaking skills so that I could become a better communicator. After taking several public speaking courses, I was doing so well that I chose to participate in a public speaking competition. It was my first one. There I was, speaking in English, competing with Americans. I felt on top of the world. I did not win the competition, but I was happy for having had the courage to take that risk.

That awesome feeling did not last long. Soon after my speech was over, one of the program leaders walked over to me and said, "May I give you some feedback?" With a big smile on my face, expecting some words of recognition for taking the risk to participate in my first public speaking competition, I said, "Suuuuuure." He looked at me and said, "I could not understand a word you were saying. You better lose the accent, or get out of the speaking business. Do your audience a favor and don't speak." His words were like a knife going through my stomach. I was shocked, angry, and disappointed. For the next few days, I could hear his words pounding in my head, again and again: "Lose the accent." "Lose the accent." " . . .the accent" . . . "accent" . . . .

Figuring that one out took me awhile, but I finally realized that my accent was part of who I was; it was my trademark. English is not my first language. Therefore, I have an accent. Some people believe that America is a "melting pot"—that we should eliminate our own culture and "fit in." But I have learned differently. We are people, and people don't melt. America is a land of diversity, where every culture is *uniquely* represented, where every way of thinking is freely expressed, and every accent is powerfully heard.

I then remembered a plaque in my Spanish teacher's office that read, "Everyone who has an accent is someone special because he speaks at least one more language." Sometimes people react to an accent as they do to a mission statement. Once an accent is known to others, people will be divided between those who will accept it and even enjoy it, and those who will not. Therefore, just because of one trait I have, some people will accept me, and some will not. That is okay. I also learned that, when I am authentically expressing myself, I have to expect opposition. That is also okay. A new breakthrough! *My rainbow was now highlighted with the color indigo.*

Journaling for consciousness: Have you found yourself in a situation where you were not accepted? Did that stop you from freely expressing your true self? How can that experience empower you to be more of who you are?

Violet: Truth – Seeking a New Level

Through all my cross-cultural experiences, there was another line of consciousness being tested: my faith in God. As I became so close to folks from around the world, I was also exposed to their religions . . . Islam, Buddhism, Hinduism, New Age, Atheism. Having been raised Christian, and taught that my religion was the ultimate one, I was pretty set on what was the "proper" way to have a meaningful relationship with God. For a long time, I would avoid the religion subject, as I did not want to put myself in a place where my faith would be questioned. Therefore, I allowed religion and faith to be a point of difference between us.

Until one day I decided to give their beliefs a chance, and took the step to learn their faiths. As I started to learn from them, I realized that our beliefs were not that different. We had different models, but the same faith in God. Yes, that opened the door for my faith to be questioned, but I also learned that *truth* does not go away when questioned. When we question truth, we get more truth. Learning other religions has allowed my faith in God to increase and my relationship with Him to become stronger than ever before. I have become a much better Christian, much more able to love and accept others unconditionally, like Christ did. *The color violet was added to my rainbow.*

Journaling for consciousness: What do you mean by *truth*? Do you ever take the time to question your truth and seek a new level of truth?

White: Authenticity – Bringing It All Together

With each color that was added to my rainbow, I gained more power to create my life as a true expression of who I am. From each experience, I learned to detach from relative values and beliefs, and was freed to create my own reality, which gradually becomes closer and closer to an absolute one. I still have many colors to add to my rainbow . . . pink, cyan, silver, magenta, aqua, gold . . . as a true rainbow has an infinite number of colors, resulting in the color white, the sum of all the colors. I often wonder how many colors there are in God's rainbow. He must have *all* the colors. He can see everything with absolute accuracy, and that is why He was able to create the universe with such a magnificent degree of precision. That is the ultimate Creative Intelligence! As I continue to grow and add new colors to my rainbow, I become more like God, and become a better expression of His intelligence on this earth.

I now invite you to look out into the world. Take the risk, get out there, and embrace diversity, whether it is cultural diversity or another type of diversity. Learn from others and allow your perceptions to be challenged. Take time to look at the rainbow of *your* consciousness, and ask yourself, "How many colors am I still missing?" Look beyond the expectations of others and take charge of your life. Take the risk, step out of the box, and create something new. Have the courage to create something that is an authentic expression of your true self. When faced with a challenge, be ready to look beyond it, focus on the lesson that you are about to learn, welcome the wisdom that comes with it . . . **and a new color will be added to *your* rainbow.**

About
Aline Vieira

As a Life Coach, speaker, and writer, Aline Vieira uses creativity and intuition to empower international professional women to create a heart-driven life and career in the United States. Aline arrived from Brazil in 1987 with the dream of creating a better life in America. Almost twenty years later, with many blessings received, many successes achieved, and having adapted to the American culture, both corporate and non-corporate, she is now helping other international women accomplish the same. In 2002, she founded Authentic Strategies with the aim of providing personal and professional development coaching services to the international professional women in America.

Aline is dedicated to empowering her clients to become more rooted in their "true selves," guiding them to experience the clarity and realization of their authentic life purpose, vision, and passion. Her goal is to inspire these women to successfully contribute to the American market in a fulfilling and meaningful manner while embracing their unique background. Her coaching model revolves around helping her clients first come to a point where they can fully articulate what their life purpose is, and then supporting them to create a fulfilling life and career based on that life purpose.

Aline believes that what the international professional women in America have to offer this country is as great as what they have to gain from it, and she wants to facilitate that process. "We came to this country with so many dreams of what we can accomplish for our own good," she says. "However, let's not forget how much we have to offer back in terms of culture, wisdom, and life experience. We came here for a purpose; we came here to make a difference."

Aline has an extensive educational background. She earned her bachelor's degree from Truman State University, in Kirksville, Missouri. Her personal growth journey has been highlighted and strengthened by some of the most powerful courses available in North America, including, Zig Ziglar's *Over The Top*, Stephen Covey's *Seven Habits of Highly Effective People*, and *The Dale Carnegie Course*. Her desire to continue improving her coaching skills drove her to IPEC—Institute of Professional Empowerment Coaching, from which she graduated in 2004 as a Professional Empowerment Coach. IPEC was founded by Dr. Bruce Schneider, the author of the book, *Relax, You Are Already Perfect*. Aline chose IPEC as the coaching community of her choice for its commitment to developing the client as a perfect being who is ready to step into the next level, the level of excellence.

To contact Aline, email avieira@authenticstrategies.com or for more information, visit www.AuthenticStrategies.com.

Designing Your Success: Intelligently Creating Your Life

By Denise Braunstein

Assess the Situation

"Stop! Don't run or I'll shoot!" Once again, the police were trying to catch a cocaine dealer who had just robbed the pharmacy near my home. Between January and February 1988, that store had been raided four times. "Twice a month... Not such a bad average," I thought to myself, considering the place was Rio de Janeiro, Brazil.

For the past three decades, Brazil has suffered with economic difficulty and political turmoil. Its economy has stagnated under the burden of inflation, coupled with loads of foreign debt and widespread corruption.

When international interest rates rose out of control in the late 70's and early 80's, Brazil's highly indebted state-centered economy went broke. Citizens experienced a recession, with exponential inflation rates that grew as high as three thousand percent in one year (1989), an average inflation of 34 percent per month. In spite of many attempts to restore a healthier economy, the situation was disastrous and desperation set in the hearts of most Brazilians. Urban violence, poverty, kidnappings, and drug trafficking escalated to dangerous proportions. People considered leaving the country, but most didn't, hoping that the situation would get better one day. Only a very few had the audacity to dream of creating a better life for themselves and their families, no matter what, even if this meant changing everything, going to another country, starting all over again. The light at the end of the tunnel was somewhere else for one family living in Rio for almost a century: my own.

My family has deep roots in Brazil. My ancestors mostly arrived from Europe over one hundred years ago, fleeing from the dangers of war and persecution. Brazil, with its wide golden gates, has always embraced immigrants. It is one of the most diverse, beautiful, and exciting countries in the world. Who has not heard of my beloved Rio de Janeiro—a breathtaking, cosmopolitan, pulsating, unique, colorful, intense city—with its famous Copacabana and Ipanema beaches contrasting its spectacular mountains, with its awe-inspiring Carnaval, and the contagious warmth of its people?

Like so many kids throughout the world, I had dreamed of visiting Disneyland in California (at a time when Orlando's attractions in Florida were not even on the map!). I can still remember when I was eleven years old and my parents told me that they had a surprise for me: "We have airplane tickets for a family vacation to the United States!" I was ecstatic! Tears of pure joy rolled down my cheeks, while I was jumping all over the family room. We had a fantastic trip, which increased even more my fascination with the United States and the American people. Over the next years, I kept returning to the U.S. to visit other parts of the country. I learned to speak English, and immersed myself in the American culture. My family hosted an American exchange student, and my husband and I even chose the States for our honeymoon. Then, during Brazil's hyperinflation crisis, my ever-growing dreams of going to America reached a new maturity.

Build Your Success Team

Day after day, the overwhelming stress of living in Brazil kept inching closer to my threshold of tolerance. I had lost perspective of what a peaceful life was by drifting for so long in my country's chaotic situation. It is often difficult to see what is beyond the limits of our comfort zone. My energy was being drained into an abyss of frustrations and fears, instead of moving me toward a compelling future. I was not being the best I could be. There was no action plan for what I wanted in my future. I was not enjoying all that life had to offer. Oh, how far I was from my personal definition of success! I knew that I needed to change dramatically, and shift my paradigms if I wanted to continue to progress in my personal and professional life. Although my husband and I had been supporting each other during those trying times, I felt we were both submerged under similar perspectives.

An enlightening idea came to me then. I would hire someone to be part of my winning team—a coach—to help me live my highest standards of an ideal life. Working with a coach was a crucial strategic decision because I finally had a person who did not have her own agenda, was detached enough from the outcome, was totally committed to support me, and could bring fresh perspectives to the table.

Initially, our partnership was focused on gaining clarity about my situation, similar to the way I coach my clients. Powerful and thought-provoking questions evoked an abundance of insights. What were the differences between my present state (where I was) and my desired state (where I wanted to be)? How did I want to live my life? What were my dreams and life purpose? What was my personal definition of success? Was I living within the boundaries of my values system? Engaging in the coaching process ignited a monumental fire within my being, helping me reprogram my own questioning to produce the most positive and efficient responses. What did I genuinely desire to experience? How could I make the greatest difference in my life and in the lives of my family? How could I leverage my strengths?

Take Full Responsibility

Soon I realized that it was an absolute necessity to take full responsibility for the nature and quality of my life and results. I had endured enough—enough years spent placing my dreams on the side, enough struggling with living in a threatening environment. Enough! Did I really want to wait passively for external conditions, beyond my control, to eventually change for the better? No! I had been letting life happen to me, hoping for the best, instead of carefully *choosing* how to live my best life! Choice and responsibility were the seeds of what became my program for helping others find direction in their lives: Designing Your Success Coaching. I started with a big dream—to carefully design a successful, fulfilling, and joyful experience for my life. My enriching experience with my coach inspired me to want to share this process with others to implement in their own lives.

The idea of designing my success started to take shape. Recapturing many memories and emotions from my past and reviewing the path I had taken up to that point, I realized that everything in my past had actually been perfect. Everything had led to that exact transformative moment. Each and every choice I had made in the past resulted in my experience of that present second. Everyone—including me—had always done the best they could with what they knew at the time. Back to the drawing board. I started to consciously design the next part of my life, doing more of what was working, doing less of what wasn't, and trying on new behaviors to see if they would produce better results. How thrilling it was to grab an inviting canvas—my destiny—and paint it with the colors I chose for my success and happiness!

Courage to Change

It was time to make one of the most significant decisions of my life. The deeper the crisis, the deeper the questions raised and the tougher the decisions to make. Either I decide what I want, or it will be decided for me. Either I go for my dreams, or I'll be part of someone else's. If I wait too much, I may have to work on the bad results instead of living with the good outcomes. I was ready to take matters in my own hands and be in command of the only three things I can actually control in life: the thoughts I think, the images I visualize, and the actions I take (my behavior). If I kept on doing what I had always done, I would keep getting the same results. To get a different outcome, having to *change* was a priority.

Change involves taking risks. We run the risk of failure, being wrong, or confrontation. We run the risk of disapproval, ridicule, judgment, rejection, or even loneliness. Change might be difficult, confusing, and uncomfortable; it is rarely smooth or predictable.

In fact, it is often an emotional struggle. Most people try to avoid it, and my husband was no exception. At first, he was reluctant about my ideas of change. He was fearful and resistant. It seemed easier for him to stay where we were, and just cope with the consequences. Those were the known risks! For me, a major change was a tremendous challenge as well, but I would be ready to overcome any obstacle coming my way. A change was also a new opportunity with greater options and potential. It was a very conscious decision, requiring discipline, determination, positive attitude, and a great support system (including my coach).

Believe It Is Possible

Screaming voices of my soul kept emerging—oh, those subdued dreams, longing to be taken seriously! How could I ignore them? Tough confrontations with the wants and needs of our family clarified our common and individual dreams, goals for the future, and changes to be effected. Our renewed sense of purpose refreshed us, and an enormous sense of relief took over me. Whew! There was no way I could change the problem—the quality of life in Brazil—but I could change the opportunities within the problem.

The solution we found within the opportunities was living in another country. We finally knew with all our hearts that we did not want to be spectators, waiting to see if conditions would eventually be modified in Brazil, while our dreams were forced to come to a halt indefinitely. What a waste! Talent, personality, and skill tell us what we *can* do. Motivation tells us what we *will* do. There was only one place in the world where we wanted to live—the U.S.—and we found our courage to change because we believed it was possible.

After my husband and I had come to grips with the need for change, our energy shifted as we gave up the old ways and began to focus on the next steps. Questions such as "What is it that we are losing?" "What patterns are being disrupted?" "What are we gaining?" "What resources do we have?" were very helpful to take stock of our situation. Awareness of our losses were heartbreaking: the loving connectedness we shared with family and friends in frequent reunions; restaurants, shopping malls, and theaters we used to go to in Rio; the social club we belonged to that was located on an island; maids to cook, press, and clean for us; our home designed and built to our taste (which overlooked the Atlantic Ocean at Copacabana Beach), and Sugar Loaf mountain greeting us everyday we went to work. How could we leave so much behind?

After establishing a starting point and end-point, it was only a matter of how and when to get there. I knew there would be a brutal resistance from my loved ones, and I would have to swim against the current, as they did not approve of my idea to leave the country. Sometimes, my inner critic was overpowering: "I don't think I can do that." "This relocating idea sounds crazy." "It's never going to happen." "It's easier to just forget this whole thing." At the same time, I kept reminding myself: "Life is not a dress rehearsal, it's the real thing. Am I happy with the way things are?"

Uncover and Develop Your Brilliance

We all have dreams, desires, wishes, aspirations—or had them at one point before they were suffocated by chores, routine, unfulfilling careers, a chaotic country. Most of us dream of succeeding professionally, finding love, having a family, getting rich, traveling, perhaps engaging in a social cause, changing the world, having a better life somehow. In other words, being successful according to our own definitions! But success does not always equate to happiness.

In my coaching practice, I have known many clients who first come to me seeking help to balance and improve many areas of their lives—relationships, work, business, career, productivity, environment, health, wellbeing, personal development, stress management, and so on. Some of those clients have achieved extreme levels of success, including being rich and famous. But they are often stressed, overworked, overwhelmed, and unhappy. Chains of self-limiting beliefs anchor their goals to the bottom, far below what they are truly capable of accomplishing, not even reflecting their integral needs, wants, and values. Other clients are enslaved by their own bureaucracy, imagining that one day things will be different if they get more money, if their kids behave, if their organizations thrive, if...if...if... It is not unusual to hear those clients having the illusion that happiness and quality of life can only be reached outside of work or outside their daily lives —perhaps on the weekends or on their next vacation. During so many years of experience as a professional coach, and as a clinical and organizational psychologist, I have witnessed the direct relationship between responsibility, control, and happiness. The more responsibility that people accept, the more of an internal locus of control they develop and the more powerful, confident, and happy they feel.

When my clients are supported to uncover and develop their unlimited brilliance, they take full responsibility for their lives (no blaming and no excuses), and take intelligent, consistent actions toward their goals. I am always delighted to witness the restoration of their lost sparkle, after we remove the many layers of dust accumulated throughout the years. It is celebration time when they discover their personal power, when we bring forth unseen possibilities, and we get results! Together, our team synergy becomes more than the sum of its parts.

How about you, dear reader? Have you thoroughly evaluated your life to see where you are and where you are heading? Are you living and enjoying every moment? Or perhaps you are just going through the motions? Do you keep telling yourself that one day your life will really start? Have you ever considered how your life will be in ten or twenty years, if you keep going in the same tracks? Will you wake up beside the one you love? Will you go to work where you desire? Will you be doing what you like? Living where you want? Relating to the friends you love? The most important question is to ask yourself is how you want to live your life and to what extent that is actually happening right now. If "not enough" is the answer representing the gap between your present life and your ideal life, then you have some exciting changes to make. Your new life adventure could be starting right now!

S.M.A.R.T. Goal-Setting Power

Once I knew my life purpose, determined my vision, and clarified what my true needs and desires were, I had to convert them into specific, measurable goals and objectives and then act on them with the certainty that I would achieve them. Goal setting has been so powerful to me, that the very act of thinking about my goals has made me happy, even before I have taken any step to achieve them. Most importantly, if I do not write my goals down, they remain only a wish or a preference. During those days of preparation to relocate to America, one of my first goals was to maintain an up-to-date written list of my goals and another list of to-dos by my bedside. Examples? Instead of writing "I would like to go to the States", I wrote "I will fly from Rio to Miami with my husband and two sons, by January of next year." In my to-do list, there were daily tasks, such as "separate the items to be donated." That laser focus, like a guided missile, directed me to move unerringly toward my goals.

The process of setting S.M.A.R.T. (Specific, Measurable, Attainable, Realistic, and Timely) goals, working toward them daily, and ultimately achieving them, is paramount to happiness and success. A new state of mind propels us to dream big, to feel peaceful, to be challenged up to our highest potential, and to struggle less.

The next goal was to reframe all aspects of the situation to fit my objectives. I consciously embraced the constructive perspectives needed to create great results. Instead of struggling with the negatives, the situation could be dealt with easier (and with a lot more fun) if the focus was on the positives. Thus, I shifted from fearing what I would have to leave behind in Rio to being thrilled about what I would gain by relocating to the U.S.; from leaving the security of the well-known to embracing what I would still discover; from feeling stuck to feeling grateful. I could use my energy to create the momentum needed to take us forward, or use it to drown myself in worries. It was a powerful thing to choose the meanings I was giving to my experiences, choosing my reactions to those personal perceptions, taking greater control over my life.

Create an Exciting Visual

Experience had shown me that to solidify my dreams I must intensively visualize with all my senses exactly what I wanted, as if I had already achieved it. Then, I needed to rehearse my visualization by practicing the desired outcomes with frequent intensity to create new neurological pathways in my brain. One of the best ways I found to create this compelling picture of my ideal life, to involve my entire mind and body, and to engage the right and left sides of my brain, was to cut out inspiring pictures from magazines and produce a collage. I looked for pictures of places that reminded me of my dreams (home, environment, work, etc.), people I wanted to be with, activities I would do, expressions of feelings I would have, sounds I would hear, things that would evoke my senses of taste and smell, songs that would create that perfect climate. While I chose to visualize my dream through a collage, others may prefer to paint or draw the images associated with their dreams. If you like photography, you can take your own pictures, or make a little video, or even just use a tape-recorder to add more depth and reality to your vision. Be creative!

My finished collage was a detailed and tangible expression of the vision I was passionate to ignite. I could see my family and myself living happily in a beautiful and peaceful house in South Florida. The smell of fresh and perfumed air from trees and gardens surrounding my home was delicious. The dog I would finally have was playing catch with me in the backyard. The absence of noisy traffic jams was pure joy to my heart. What a relief to leave the windows of my car open while stopping at a red light, without fear of being assaulted! How inspiring to see my kids go to school with a variety of opportunities to fulfill their potential, with clubs and activities to choose from, so that it would be easier for them to follow their own dreams. The sweet memories I had from many other trips to the U.S. added to the liveliness of those visualizations. On Independence Day, we would be watching a spectacular fireworks show. My house would be covered in orange and black decorations for Halloween, while my kids would have a blast in their first trick-or-treating experience. So much fun! Chocolate chip pancakes at IHOP were just a corner away... Mmmm! My vision of success and happiness in America was so compelling that I had goose bumps of hope and excitement. I could not wait to get going!

Take the Plunge

In my experience, I have found that the one thing that seems to separate successful people from everyone else is that the successful ones take action. They simply do what has to be done. Once they have a plan, they get into motion. Even if they don't start perfectly, they learn from their mistakes, make the necessary corrections, and keep taking action, building momentum, until they finally produce their desired outcomes. The number of people who get bogged down in analyzing, planning, and organizing when they only need to take the plunge and act immediately, is surprising. In fact, I had spent lots of extra time analyzing and worrying about things that could go wrong in our moving. "What if we don't adapt in the States? What if the kids don't like the new schools? What if we miss our family and friends in Brazil terribly? What if my husband and I won't find suitable work?" More and more worrisome questions I had no way to answer! Then, I realized that inaction and fears took away from the time I could be doing what was really necessary. Accepting what might happen, whether in success or failure, freed me to act upon what I could do, instead of what I could not do.

Instead of sitting on the sidelines reflecting and contemplating, I created action, which in turn let those around me know that I was serious in my intention, attracting more resources and support. As expected, the practical part and logistics of the move were overwhelming—paperwork, visas, allocation of resources, what will be left, what will go. Emotions, in a mix of anxiety, sadness, hopes, and joy, were intensifying. Imagining that saying farewell to our family at the airport on the day we were moving would be extremely difficult and nerve-wracking was easy to do. To support my family, I helped them to visualize ourselves at the airport, at the moment of departure from our loved ones. How would their feelings be dealt with? I saw myself as I wanted to be: composed, calm, in charge of my emotions. I would hug and kiss each one of them with intense love, knowing that it would not be the last time, and that I would see them many other times in the future.

Ready. Set. Launch.

When the day of departure finally came, the tough moment breezed through, unveiling itself as I had prepared my family and myself to feel. The kids were looking forward to an incredible new adventure, especially to live near Disney World (only three hours away by car). My husband and I were prepared to have a smooth transition from one lifestyle to another. But there was one step I overlooked: when the flight attendant slammed the door of the plane. Bam! An unforgettable chilling moment of truth, the umbilical cord being cut right there, crashing painfully into my face. A mixture of profound sadness and extraordinary excitement flooded my being, as I realized that life, as I knew it, had changed forever. Engines started and the plane moved away from Rio's International Airport, toward the runway. Four, three, two, one…We were holding hands, exchanging meaningful glances… And lifted off to our new lives!

The first month flew by without major incidents, except for that first day when we burned a store-bought pizza inside our new oven, and I had to call the firemen. Simple, if it were not for the dense smoke spreading all over the kitchen and house, if we could find a phone in that new home, and if we knew how to shut off the shrieking alarm system to talk with the 911 staff. After all was safe, a fireman invited my kids to visit their firetruck, and asked me, "Which kind of pizza did you have? Was it pepperoni?" They had made a funny bet between themselves, and their warmth, wit, support, and efficient help was the best American welcome message I could hope for. That moment etched my soul with sublime tears of joy just like when my parents first told me that I would visit the States. As I looked at those smiling firemen, I realized that I had already started to live my dream! Yes, it was pepperoni, the best pizza I have ever—never—had.

Enjoy the High!

Looking back at this journey, from envisioning my life in America, to actually having lived in sunny Florida for more than a decade, I see that the process of designing a great life is always a worthwhile journey into the unknown, no matter how difficult it may be. I can say that I have achieved many of my dreams, have been living my life purpose, and will certainly continue to do so. I hope you are inspired and empowered by an intense, burning desire to manifest your highest vision—your true destiny—in a sea of love and joy.

Starting with a full awareness of my situation in Rio, I made a conscious decision to do whatever was necessary to change that situation, gathering strength, support, focus, and momentum to propel this massive plane on full speed ahead. Those challenging experiences laid the foundation for the new level of brilliance that my family and I now enjoy. My oldest son is now a Harvard-graduated physicist, mathematician, and musician; my younger son is also a thriving shining star as he finishes high school. My husband has a great business, and I have a very successful and fulfilling coaching practice. Most important: we are all deeply happy with our lives!

You, too, can apply similar concepts in your own life. They have worked for me and for countless others. You and you alone are responsible for taking the actions to create the life of your dreams. If you choose to consistently engage your efforts, you will produce powerful results. How are you creatively and intelligently designing your success?

My heartfelt gratitude goes to all the people who were or are part of my successful and happy journey and to those whose successful and happy journeys I have also been a part of in some way.

About
Denise Braunstein

As a Professional Life and Business Coach, Denise Braunstein, M.A., C.L.S., C.U.G., is devoted to supporting individuals, teams, and businesses design and achieve substantial levels of success, productivity, and happiness in an effortless way. Denise followed her lifetime calling to develop human potential in others and in her self, by first becoming a Clinical and Industrial Psychologist in 1983. Her passionate commitment to professional excellence led to her utmost dream of being a masterful national and international Coach.

Designing Your Success Coaching (DYS) was founded by Denise in 1999 to better suit the needs of her clients, including professionals, entrepreneurs, business owners, executives, employees, and homemakers, from all backgrounds and nationalities. Denise's extensive mix of experiences, fluency in English and Portuguese, continuous learning, blended with her cutting-edge coaching approach, humor and enthusiasm, distinguishes herself as a results-oriented, compassionate, and holistic Life, Career, and Business Coach. She is a Certified Life Strategist and Planner, graduate of Coach University, founding member of the International Association of Coaches (IAC), member of the International Coach Federation (ICF), CoachVille, and other coaching organizations.

To contact Denise, email Denise@DesigningYourSuccess. com, call 954-344-6749, or visit www.DesigningYourSuccess.com.

Transform Your Pain Into Passion

By Wendi Kovar

In January 2004, I crossed the finish line at the P.F. Chang Rock-n-Roll Marathon in the desert outside Phoenix. The feeling I had was like finding my way back home from the Land of Oz. Because running those 26 miles was really the end of a journey that I had begun sixteen years earlier in another desert in California. It was there that I first became aware of Creative Intelligence, my catalyst and my guide for the personal transformation ultimately reflected in the miles I ran in the healing air of the Arizona desert.

My first conscious contact with Creative Intelligence came in the Meditation Room of the Betty Ford Center outside of Palm Springs, California. For me, Creative Intelligence is a loving energy force in the Universe that allows the act of creation to occur naturally. This energy resides in the heart and quietly speaks the truth based in love. Creative Intelligence is rivaled by another force that I call Destructive Intelligence, which reflects lower frequency energy (self-doubt, anger, jealousy, etc.) that occupies your mind. While Creative Intelligence's voice is loving and compassionate, the voice of Destructive Intelligence is loud and critical. Although both forces reside in each of us, you can choose which one will guide your life. You can choose to live in the pain that Destructive Intelligence causes, or you can choose to use that pain as a seed to access your truth, allowing Creative Intelligence to help you transform your life.

When I entered the Betty Ford Center, I was only vaguely aware of the power of Creative Intelligence. At the age of 28, I finally realized that I was losing my ten-year struggle to drink alcohol like a "normal" person. I willingly entered the Center, wide-eyed, waving the white flag of surrender. I admittedly had lost the battle, but deep inside I heard, "Now, perhaps, you will win the war."

The battle I am referring to was a life that looked good on the outside, but was empty on the inside. There was a gaping hole in my soul where all the good esteeming stuff slowly seeped out. The emptier I became, the harder I tried to make the outside appear good. I marched around to the mantra in my head, *"If you look good, you feel good; if you feel good, you do good; if you do good, you are good."* I was always in some sort of action, too busy to feel or really contemplate what values my actions were or were not honoring in my life.

In my mind, my life had gone perfectly according to my plan—until it didn't. I had married my high school sweetheart, I had become a partial owner and corporate treasurer in our third-generation family business, I had purchased a home by the time I was twenty, and I had completed my college education majoring in Business and Psychology. I adored my husband, whom I called "The Bear." The only missing piece was having a family of our own. That plan simply was not happening, regardless of our efforts, medical procedures, and our loving family support. Eight years of invasive infertility treatments and many disappointments can destroy the best of unions. It certainly took its toll on us.

We slowly watched pain and disappointment move into our beautiful home with the spectacular view of Puget Sound. Although the scene was beautiful from the inside, those disappointments began to damage the most important point of view—how we saw each other. Alcohol eased my pain and made life tolerable, allowing me to put on my happy-face mask that probably fooled no one but me. Apparently the pain became too much because on a river rafting trip with friends in the summer of 1988, the raging Rogue River in southern Oregon almost swept my sorry soul away.

I have no recollection of what happened. I was in what they call "an alcoholic blackout." After everyone had retired to their tents following an evening of drinking, I started to stagger into the river in the dead of night, my own darkness melding perfectly into the eve, ready to relieve myself from my emotional pain. Miraculously, an earth angel in the form of another rafter pulled me out of the river and watched me stumble my way back to my tent.

I bleakly awoke in the morning, unaware of how I managed to coat myself in sand and grit. When I finally left our tent, one of the river guides handed me a life preserver and told me I had to unite with it for the remainder of the trip. It was very humiliating, but somehow we all turned it into a joke.

Everyone laughed it off except The Bear. He took me aside and said, "That wasn't funny. You've been asking me for a while if I think you have a drinking problem and now the answer is affirmative. I want to know what you are going to do about it?" He didn't need to threaten me with leaving, because I knew he had enough self respect to do just that; that was one of the things I admired so much about him. I knew what I had to do, and so I thought of the best treatment center I could and decided on the Betty Ford Center. I have never regretted that life saving decision and I am forever grateful for my second chance at life. So, there I was at Betty Ford...

My first assignment was to visit the Meditation Room and attempt to make contact with my "Higher Power." I settled myself and gazed out the enormous picture window. I couldn't believe that I was actually in an alcohol and drug treatment facility for thirty days! I had never gone more than twenty-one days without drinking in fourteen years.

I decided to heed the advice of taking it "one day at a time" and allowed my creative denial system to tell myself I was at "Camp Betty." I sat in the Meditation Room with no idea how to meditate. I wondered if I was supposed to hum? I looked over at the only other person there and noticed she was being very quiet and still so I opted for silence as well. I waited. Nothing. I focused on a tree branch and I silently declared, "God, if you are there, please show me a sign. Like, make this branch move, just a little." Still nothing. I sat there for the designated twenty-five minutes and was disappointed to have witnessed no burning bushes or even a branch wiggle.

I hesitantly started back to my new home, and the other woman from the Meditation Room said "Hi" in a thick and endearing southern drawl. She was five days more seasoned than me, and graciously answered my numerous questions in her humorous and relaxed way. I risked asking her about the meditation. "Did you feel anything in there?" I ventured, sheepishly. She responded, "I declared that if there is a Higher Power up there, please make that branch on the tree move. It didn't."

Although our H.P. had not moved the branch as requested, it moved our hearts together in that Meditation Room. We became kindred spirits, supporting each other day after day. We laughed hysterically, cried uncontrollably, ranted, raved, and gloriously laughed again. I called her Red Foot; she called me Sweet Wendi. The tears of truth roll down my cheeks as I recall her spirit.

That is how my Higher Power showed up for me at Camp Betty. Everyday an amazing connection would occur, and never what I expected. What I learned was that my Higher Power, God, Creative Intelligence, the name is unimportant, had a plan that was far superior to my own. I simply had to be open to the messages and be willing to do things out of my comfort zone. I literally chose to "trust the process and stay in the moment."

On the day of my "Goodbye Ceremony," where you share your hope and wisdom with the frightened newcomers, Creative Intelligence made a grand appearance that I regarded as a personal graduation gift. I had planned to read the poem "The Man in the Mirror." Before the ceremony, I stopped in the Camp Store and discovered a poem entitled "The Gal in the Glass." It was the same as the "Man in the Mirror' except in feminine form. It had not been in the store before. How did this poem come to be in the store on **my day**? I chose to believe it was Creative Intelligence's way of making me aware of its presence. Being aware of this force and the role it plays, both large and small, has made all the difference to me.

The Gal in the Glass

> When you get what you want in your struggle for self
> and the world makes you queen for a day,
> just go to a mirror and look at yourself
> and see what that gal has to say.
> For it isn't your husband or family or friend
> whose judgment upon you must pass,

the gal whose verdict counts most in the end
is the one looking back from the glass.
Some people may think you a straight-shootin' chum
and call you a person of place,
but the gal in the glass says you're only a bum
if you can't look her straight in the face.
She's the one to please, never mind all the rest
for she's with you clear up to the end
and you've passed your most dangerous, difficult test
if the gal in the glass is your friend.
You may fool the whole world down the pathway of years
and get pats on the back as you pass,
but your final reward will be heartache and tears
if you've cheated the gal in the glass.
~Author Anonymous

I graduated from the Betty Ford Center with honors. I have honored myself with sixteen years of sobriety thanks to the quality information I received, the intense involvement with others who were courageously confronting their disease, and the absolute knowledge that for me, drinking equals death. I keep it simple.

The advice I was given from my councilors was that I leave the family business that I had worked at for fourteen years. I heeded their advice and decided to enter the Real Estate business, as it complimented my husband's architectural and construction business. It proved to be a positive decision in every way.

Tackling my addiction to alcohol was a breeze compared to dealing with my dependence on The Bear. I literally didn't think that I could live without him. I didn't want to anyway. After ten years of marriage and seventeen years of being in a committed relationship, The Bear walked out on me, exclaiming that "Something is very wrong and you will never leave." He was right, on both accounts. I was too afraid to leave. I believed I needed his intellect, love, and humor to be complete; I didn't trust that I had those qualities without him.

When The Bear left, I was lost. I thought I needed him to complete me, to fill in my many gaps. He did the thinking, I did the feeling; it was our unspoken agreement. Yet deep down, I knew he was right; there was something very wrong, and I just did not want it to be so. I put on my designer coat of denial and plunged into work and exercise so that I had no time to feel. *"If I look good I feel good; if I feel good I do good; if I do good I am good."*

At The Bear's departure, I didn't even cry; it literally hurt too much. When the pain and confusion started tempting me to drink, I returned to the desert for a five-day intense program to get a grip on my life that, once again, was not going according to my plan.

The healing effects of the dry desert helped me understand that I was not in a healthy marriage and that something had to change immediately. I called The Bear for a meeting. I would have bet my life that we were going to get back together that night. Creative Intelligence had another plan.

Shortly into our talk, our rambunctious dog knocked a granite coffee table onto my bare toe. I hopped around the yard on one foot trying to relieve the excruciating pain while The Bear called the nearest medical clinic. The doctor on call said to come right away and that he would wait. My wildest dreams could not have prepared me for what was about to happen. As The Bear helped me hobble into the clinic, the most captivating human being I had ever laid eyes on greeted us. I must have been staring because he asked if he knew me. I said, "No," but my mind screamed, "I'd sure love to know you!" The doctor took my injured foot in his hand to examine it. With that one touch, I felt no pain. My entire body broke out in goose bumps. I was astonished and amazed at the intensity of my feelings for this man who was a total stranger, although something about him seemed so safe and so familiar.

My toe was broken, so I had to return to the clinic for four consecutive visits. At the last visit, I asked the doctor if he would be my permanent physician. He was surprised I didn't have one, so I explained that I had seen only fertility doctors for the past eight years. Since I was separated, I wouldn't be seeing them anymore, and now needed a physician.

That night I called a friend who was a nurse at the clinic. I asked her about the good doctor. A few minutes after we talked, the doctor called the same nurse. He realized that he had made a mistake by agreeing to be my physician. He was attracted to me and it would be a breach of his professional ethics to see me as a patient. She laughed and told him about my phone call. Due to professional ethics, I had to call him. We met for dinner and have been inseparable ever since.

I warned him at the beginning that I was not much of a catch. After all, I was an infertile, soon-to-be-divorced, recovering alcoholic. He gave me this all-knowing smile and replied, "You are not infertile." Time has proved him right—our marital union has been blessed with two miraculous children, conceived without any medical assistance, just Creative Intelligence. By opening myself to possibilities, and aligning myself with someone who had complete faith in my ability to be a mother, I became a mother.

Michael is my soul mate. He is an ideal husband, friend, lover, and father. He is my proof that Creative Intelligence does exist and that I am loved. He is my reward for living a consciously healthy life and my reminder that there is nothing to fear.

A few years after Michael and I were married and our children were born, I realized another major change was imminent. I was no longer fulfilled working in the Real Estate industry. My new calling was to become a Professional Life Coach, where I partner with people in living their lives according to their values and manifesting their dreams into reality.

To be able to walk my talk, I found it was necessary for me to eliminate the emotional baggage I was still lugging around. Recognizing the desert is a healing place for me, I registered for the P.F. Chang Rock-n-Roll Marathon in Phoenix, Arizona. My enthusiasm inspired my sisters-in-law to join me.

The energy of the marathon crowd and the 27,000 runners was electric. I knew one thing for certain; this was my first and last marathon, and I announced it to my sisters-in-law as we waited at the starting line.

As I waited for that starting gun with my Emerald Sisters from the Emerald City, I was magically reminded of Dorothy's travels in the Wizard of Oz. Our journeys were very similar. I had, one-by-one, found the parts of me that were missing: intellectually (brain), emotionally (heart), and now physically (courage). Running this marathon was leading me home to my complete self. I glanced downward and imagined my Nike's had transformed into stunning ruby slippers.

The gun was fired as we took off in a dense crowd of color and anticipation. I focused on my intention to leave my past behind and suddenly I heard the faint notes of the first song being played: "Brown-Eyed Girl" by Van Morrison, my ex-husband's favorite song. I mustered all the energy I could and ran as fast as possible through those notes of emotional pain. This person whom I loved deeply represented the Scarecrow, Tin Man, and Lion in my life. I believed I needed his intellect, love, and courage to be complete.

I was deeply sorry for all the unconscious mistakes I made and hoped he forgave me as I forgave him. I sincerely prayed that he was as happy in his new life with his wife and biological children (That's right!) as I was in mine. I purposely blasted out that pain residue so that I could be more present in my current love life. Free at last, I knew I had all the love I needed within me.

My sweet sisters-in-law were unaware of the internal marathon I was simultaneously running. They became the "Glenda the Good Witch" character. I felt loved and positively supported, always. I was running and consciously reinventing myself as I covered each mile, throwing away what no longer served me, revising how I viewed myself. I saw myself whole, healthy, courageous and strong. I was delighted to realize that my breath returned to normal following the first milestone.

Then the next song played. It was the favorite song of someone I had thought of as a friend, but who, in fact, undermined and betrayed me at every opportunity. This person represented The Wicked Witch. I had naively handed my ruby slippers to her, unaware of their power or the Witch's. But the ruby slippers were now firmly back on my feet. The thunder-like burst of energy I had on this mile felt victorious as I stomped the ground as hard as possible. These memories needed to go deep into the desert. As part of my goal of ridding myself of baggage, I was consciously ending unhealthy relationships, including this one. As Dorothy stated to her rival, "Be gone; you have no power here."

As the race proceeded, the band amazed me by playing songs that helped me purge my past. My tears united with the salty sweat that rolled down my face so that my crying went unnoticed. They were tears of joy, because I knew that I was reclaiming my power and emerging as my own hero, never to be a victim again. I forged through mile after mile, shedding sweat and past hurts.

When I reached Mile Twenty, the external and internal temperature was going up. Many people were dropping out of the race due to injury or fatigue. I panicked as I assessed them more fit than me. How could I continue when they could not? I realized I was experiencing an unfounded FEAR (False Evidence Appearing Real). I released my feelings of doubt and inferiority, and I focused on the runners in front of me.

I believe I was "hitting the wall" they talk about in marathon lingo, and I told my sisters I would have to slow down my pace and let them go ahead of me. I knew I needed to do this, but my Destructive Intelligence started it's barrage of insults as it labeled me a "loser" because I would not be able to cross the finish line holding hands with my sisters as I had planned.

As I tried to quiet my mind, I heard a "Voice." But this was not the Wizard of Oz telling me what I needed to make it home. It was Creative Intelligence saying, "Wendi, you did not come here to win, you came here to inspire." Goose bumps covered my body, despite the intense heat, my clue that the truth was being spoken. I looked up and saw a sign that read, "Believe." Anchored to my previous insight, they carried me to Mile Twenty-Two.

Predictably, my chattering mind started reminding me how much my knees hurt and how tired I was and I noticed my breathing was becoming labored and loud. Suddenly, a runner in front of me turned around, assessed me, and said, "You can do it; you are really strong." I thanked him and felt my power. His words carried me all the way through Mile Twenty-Three.

At the beginning of Mile Twenty-Four, I recalled the words from my Yoga instructor when we tackled a difficult pose: "Dig deep."

I dug as deep as I thought I could. I spotted a group of children enthusiastically cheering us on. I gave them all high fives. I caught their energy and it carried me to the end of Mile Twenty-Four.

At Mile Twenty-Five, I was aware of my hips like never before. They were throbbing and aching, screaming at me to slow down, better yet, to stop. Surprisingly, I heard a cry from the crowd yell, "Hey, first and last marathoner, you are almost there. You are going to make it!" The fact that someone remembered me out of all those runners filled me with a rush of energy that made me forget about my hips.

The bright sun illuminated the beginning of Mile Twenty-Six. My yellow brick road was almost at an end. I was amazed to see some of the runners begin to walk at this point and I declared, "I can do this!" I allowed the light to fill my aching body with positive energy as I reaffirmed my intention to complete this race of a lifetime. And then I saw it—the finish line. Colorful flags and balloons illuminated the end, beckoning me to cross it. I had never seen anything so compelling and I consciously transitioned my run into leaps, clicked my heels, and pushed myself to pass as many people as I could down this last leg of my dream.

Always the passive cooperator, I was now a focused competitor. From alcoholic to athlete. From infertile woman to blessed mother. From Bear to Soul Mate. From victim to victorious. From fearful to faithful. The photo capturing me crossing the finish line reflects me flying across my goal, feet in the air and Creative Intelligence as the wind beneath my wings. I felt integrated as my mind, body, and spirit celebrated this major accomplishment. Each step along that twenty-six mile path reflected the steps I had taken starting back in 1988 when I tried to drown my sorrows in the Rogue River.

I now use the memory of completing my first and last marathon as a reminder that I can accomplish anything on which I set my intention. I secretly told myself that *if* I could finish the race, my dream of writing a book would manifest. One year later, I am a contributing author in this book and nearly finished with another book that embodies my passion. Dreams do come true and you can use your pain as the fuel to feed your passion, which consequently transforms that pain into everlasting joy, sending you somewhere over your own rainbow.

Prior to consciously connecting to Creative Intelligence, I allowed fear and my Destructive Intelligence to make my life decisions. I realize I learned everything the hard way, through experience, and I had most of it backwards.

My life is now playing in full, living color. My dreams are manifesting as I allow Creative Intelligence to guide me. I am fortunate to have the career of my dreams as a Life Coach where I partner with people to find their own yellow brick road home.

All the pain I have encountered was worth the passion I now have infused in my life. All the sadness makes my joy more delightful. All the anger has given me incredible strength. All the fear has brought me undeniable faith. All the loneliness makes me a conscious partner. The infertility issue has brought me an attitude of gratitude for the gifts of my children, Alex and Rachael. My guilt has brought me forgiveness and my shame no longer exists. I am now my own best friend and I only allow people in my life who love, respect, and appreciate me. Creative Intelligence helps me discern who those people are.

My new mantra that I flow with is: *"If I am good I do good; if I do good I feel good; and if I feel good I look good."* How I appear to others is no longer my concern. I trust the guidance I am given by Creative Intelligence because even if it is not what I want to hear, it is always what I need to live my best life. I now have faith that good things happen when I align with that voice of love and wisdom. As a Life Coach, I have seen others experience the same transformation when they align themselves with Creative Intelligence and let go of their fear and pain. We are all more alike than we are different. The lessons that I and so many other people have learned can work for you too.

Anyone can transform their pain into their passion if they are rigorously honest and are willing to take action on conscious, life-affirming choices. The process is simple—and not easy. It requires a complete surrender of what is bringing you so much pain and total acceptance of "what is." From this surrendered place, you open up to Creative Intelligence and become receptive to the guidance you will be given.

Be consciously *open* to the guidance you will receive. *Recognize* Creative Intelligence's plan and do not rigidly cling to a plan that no longer works. Pain is inevitable, but suffering is optional. You can choose whether you will allow pain to bring you down or use that pain to help you grow into the best person you can be. Allow Creative Intelligence, the loving and creative source of all that is living, to guide you to your home, your passion. And by living passionately… well, there is no place like home.

Wendi's 7 Steps to Transform Pain Into Passion:

1. **Awareness** that the pain is not bringing you any gain and you are suffering. Requires: **Honesty**
2. **Acceptance** of what is causing pain; make a decision to change it. If you can't accept or change the situation, you are choosing insanity. Requires: **Conscious Choice**
3. **Surrender** to the pain. Not like a victim; surrender like a hero: "I can't handle this on my own, so I turn it over to the loving force of Creative Intelligence." Requires: **Humility**.
4. **Open yourself** to the guidance you will receive. Let go of your expectations and be willing to take action that may take you out of your comfort zone. Recognize this is Creative Intelligence's plan, not yours. Requires: **Courage**
5. **Forgive** yourself and others for your suffering. Stay out of the past, which is loaded with pain. Stay out of the future, where worry and fear reside. Requires: **Faith**
6. **Stay present** in the moment. Honor your values at all times. Do your best and let go of perfectionism and judgment. The present is God's gift to us just as the name indicates. Requires: **Awareness**
7. Develop an **Attitude of Gratitude**. This is the path to serenity and joy. It is the road less traveled and the one that makes all the difference. You continue to grow through peace rather than pain. Requires: **Honesty, Humility, Courage, Conscious Choices, Awareness, Faith**

About
Wendi Kovar

After working with a coach to find her own inner passion for life and her career, Wendi Kovar created and enjoys a thriving Personal and Executive Coaching practice on Mercer Island in Washington state. In wanting to share her experiences and education in business with others, she became a Certified Professional Coach through the Academy of Coach Training. Combining her business education from Seattle University and twenty five years of business experience, Wendi brings a valuable set of skills and tools to her work with clients. In 2005, Wendi studied with Dr. Judith Orloff in an intensive training on Positive Energy and its effects in personal and business situations.

In 2005, Wendi established The Soul Spa, located on the serene shoreline of Hood Canal of Puget Sound. In this amazing location, Wendi offers gentle yet intensive coaching where her clients experience their authentic beauty and inner wisdom. This holistic spa is about discovery, release and spiritual freedom. Wendi also specializes in addiction and codependency healing and couples coaching.

Wendi is now living her life's dream and is passionate about helping others live theirs. To contact Wendi, email coachwendi@comcast.net or call 206-310-3818.

Out of the Wound Comes the Gift

By Lydia van den Broeck

"The intuitive mind is a sacred gift and the rational mind is a faithful servant. We have created a society that honours the servant and has forgotten the gift." ~ Albert Einstein

What is Creative Intelligence? What is that emptiness that seemingly gives form to everything? What is that nothingness, the organizing principle that shapes and structures my physical body? Who is this awesome intelligence that so effortlessly orchestrates over a trillion functions in my body, digests my food, grows my nails, and knows how to distribute the nutrients that become skin cells, hair cells? Creative Intelligence is Source, Love, God, the Essence of who I am. Deep within, like a silent reflecting pool of stillness, I find that Essence. Creative Intelligence is intuition. I want to connect with this intelligence. I want to harness Its power.

We are all artists, every one of us. Our body is like a screen we project our thoughts onto. Every thought, feeling, and breath creates and molds our life into a work of art. Not a static work of art, but an ever changing, moving, expressing container of Creative Intelligence, which cannot move and express itself through a rigid body. Like a frozen river, if creativity is not expressed freely, it stagnates. The life force severs its own access to the ocean of well-being.

In a healthy, vibrant system, fresh ideas and creative thoughts are first conceived then slowly incubated. Before a new thought, a new idea, an irresistible attraction to a lover materializes, there is creative tension and fear: fear of going beyond the familiar; fear of the unknown; fear of being vulnerable; fear of being hurt or ridiculed. We leap into uncertainty, into the void. We trust. We trust that the safety net is always there. At the perfect moment, fear dissolves into joy. The gift is delivered into the world.

My gift is my story. A story of passage, a longing, an invitation for Creative Intelligence to inspire my body, my life, and to "birth" my gifts so they may serve others. This journey is my unique and individual connection to Creative Intelligence, Source, God. Through it, may you be inspired to remember your own connection to this Source of life.

I always knew that my life's work was to be a way-shower, a teacher, a healer, to bring awareness and expand consciousness. However, a light worker's work is not listed in the course curriculum at the local university.

I was raised in Europe with very traditional values. I was the invisible child. Never fitting in, I was a lonely and sad little girl. I watched my dysfunctional family perform, like actors in a play, reenacting the same story lines over and over again. I knew this was hurting them and me. I questioned "the way things were done." I questioned religion and political systems. I questioned the criminal mind set and wondered why people do the things they do. Mostly, I could feel people's energy. I could "read" their mind. I could read their "story lines" and see the absurdity of their actions. I knew that I was different, but I wanted to be like everyone else. That was safer.

At age eleven, I knew I wanted to be a teacher. Creative Intelligence would expand that to mean a spiritual teacher and healer. However, with nobody to validate me, my aspirations were ignored and I attempted even harder to be like everyone else.

Like most of us, I was raised with the belief that having a good education, being smart and of course, marrying the "right" man would set me on the path to happiness. Like most young women, I dreamed of having children, a beautiful home, and a husband who would love me forever. I believed that I had indeed met my "knight in shining armor." I left my native Belgium and moved to London, England. I spoke virtually no English but that was no obstacle to this bright and optimistic twenty year-old.

Suffering in every form exhausts the life force. I did not know that blocked energy within me would block my path in life. I did not know that my emotions needed to be released, my heart needed to be opened, my body softened. My breath could then, like a gentle breeze, find its way through my body and animate my life. Where was I leaking power? Where was my energy draining away?

About one year into my new life, I developed a headache—nothing that a couple of Tylenols couldn't fix. Tomorrow, I would surely feel better. Definitely, the day after that. I increased the medication, added Valium to the mix, then anti-depressants. No change. Life became like a funk. My world shrank to just the bare essentials. I needed sixteen hours of sleep a day. I was tired, always tired. Tired of doing too much thinking about what was causing me to feel so bad; thinking about how I could feel better; thinking about what I could do with my life if I had no headache. But the headache never went away. For fifteen long years the headache never went away. I visited doctors, chiropractors, acupuncturists, massage therapists. Sometimes, I found relief for 30 minutes or so. By the time I arrived home, the headache was back. I didn't yet know that my symptom could not just be addressed superficially. Something was trying to get my attention. No "valid" explanation besides chronic fatigue syndrome could be found as to why I felt this way. Why was I so fatigued? What was stealing my energy? What was going on with me? I kept smiling on the outside. On the inside, I cried. No one knew.

Surely the answer could be found in a textbook. Even though my ability to concentrate was minimal, I began to educate myself. As a high school dropout, I believed that education would bring me success, acclaim, and most importantly, self-worth. I studied everything I could find, from western psychology to psychoanalysis, psychotherapeutic interventions and hypnosis to eastern philosophies and comparative religion. I took up permanent residence inside my head, sure all the answers could be found there.

There is nothing to be learned. There is much to be unlearned. Intellectually-based knowledge does not open the heart, illuminate the mind, or heal the body. It has no room for emotions. It does not include the spirit—the Source of life—the Creative Intelligence that brings passion and vitality to your existence. Intellectually-based knowledge cannot repair the energy drains caused by low self-esteem, codependency, and the need to look for validation.

"No problem can be resolved at the level at which it is created," Einstein said. The greatest pain occurs when I refuse to accept, when I put up resistance to what has already happened. I stay in the wound, in the pain. Talking about it, investigating it, reading about it, and medicating it only prolongs the suffering.

I still had the headache. My ex-husband and I moved to the United States. So did the headache. I was functioning at about 15% of capacity. I had huge energy drains. Life force was pouring out of me, wasted on trying to keep myself together, trying to please and accommodate my husband. I needed to control and manipulate just to get my basic needs met. I was very angry, defensive, sad, lonely, self-absorbed, negative, judgmental.

Then I heard Marianne Williamson's words from *A Return to Love*: "When your knees finally hit the ground is not when life is over, it's when it begins." I let go. I stopped the struggle. Struggling was a huge energy drain. I realized that struggling is fear-based, ego-based. I was afraid to let go of a husband who was not available to me. His own childhood "story" had not prepared him to take a place of honor in my life. His heart was closed. I tried so hard to open it. The hardest thing to let go of is our own suffering.

The body is a reflection of your inner world. Like a map, a landscape, your body can be read. Your body introduces you and your story to the world by the way you talk, walk, hide, or avoid another's gaze. The body is a field of intelligence, a river for the God force to move through and create in Its own image and likeness. When the head and the heart are not connected, you are disconnected from this Source. You are not present. No one is home. The more you open, breathe, and invite this intelligence to move and expand from within, the more creative and the more confident you become. God is not to be found somewhere outside of yourself. God is the essence of who you are.

Tired and exhausted, but with my insatiable desire for wholeness intact, Creative Intelligence directed me to explore the basic tenets of Quantum Physics. A light bulb came on. I experienced a strange feeling in my head as if my brain were turned around. In an instant, I understood. I understood both intellectually *and* experientially, with my head *and* with my heart that my deepest nature, the essence of my being is Source, Creative Intelligence, God. When the heart truly knows, organized religion holds no appeal. I went straight to the Source within.

I read that the atom is 99.9% empty space. I believe that empty space is Creative Intelligence. By directing the power of my thoughts, this emptiness is giving shape to my body, to my life. In the words of well-known medical intuitive Caroline Myss: "Your biography becomes your biology." All childhood messages live in this "basket" called the body. You internalize and embody old messages from the culture and from your parents. Their scolding and misperceptions live in your cells. They are familiar. They resonate as truth. Paradoxically, you are then attracted to, and end up forming relationships with the partners who have embodied that same story line, that same "truth." As you think, so you create. Your thoughts give form to your body. Energy always follows thought.

Becoming conscious is learning to listen to the deeper language of the body. To fully be in your own body, to feel the life force, is the closest we can be to Creative Intelligence, God. I can shape and command this innate intelligence to create health and well being, rather than suffering and despair. The closer I align to this intelligence, the more I attract my highest good, my deepest desire. I can access the plan for my life—my own divine perfection.

Reconnecting to the flow is transformation, which can only happen through the body, not away from it. The body is like a conduit. Suffering is a good incentive to clear the flow.

I had poor boundaries. I was trying to be in love with my husband, but I was not. I denied my own desires and tolerated inappropriate behavior. I denied myself and gave away my power. Like rocks being cleared out of a riverbed, I repaired my energy drains and reclaimed my power. When the rocks are clear, the flow is steady and powerful. Energy drains become energy gains. Intuition is God's quiet whisper moving through us, expressing and creating our experience. Events, people, and circumstances materialize and support that creation.

Trying to figure out what was causing my headache was like a dog chasing its own tail. I was creating the blockage by trying to think about how I was creating it. I couldn't feel my feelings. They were too painful. The headache was a messenger—a persistent messenger that I was disconnected from my heart, from my feelings. The river between my head and heart was full of rocks. The build-up of unresolved emotions literally created a bottleneck, an energy dam. I could hardly move my neck. My vertebrae were messed up. By refusing to feel my emotions, I chose to feel physical pain. Headache pain. The healing had to come from within.

When I felt I could take no more, an invisible hand, a peaceful breath illuminated the suffering. I saw how I had severed my life force. I was given the insight, the intuition as clear as a bell. Intuition is simply deep knowing. A knowing that does not invite questions or doubt. It just is. I was made to understand that I had created this suffering. I was made to see that I could delve deep inside and find the courage to set healthy boundaries, release fear, and embrace trust. As the creative power within me was released, I knew my own resources could create a satisfying, healthy, and prosperous life. I divorced my husband and felt a deep peace inside my being. The holy breath was quietly reorganizing my structure. My posture adjusted itself, my body relaxed, my shoulders straightened, my chest expanded, my eyes cleared. I was being reborn. I remembered. I welcomed the physiological and emotional shifts. I knew there were more shifts to come.

Healing occurs at the point where you become the observer, the witness, the watcher of your thoughts, emotions, and behavior. This witness observes the story and feels the emotions without attachment. The "story lines" are repetitive, with different actors, different players. The witnessing presence illuminates the story. Different options appear, if you are willing to listen.

I had not anticipated that connecting with Creative Intelligence, to allow the God Force to fully flow through me, means releasing control. Control of how I thought life "should" turn out.

Like most of humanity I believed that having life in control, having all my ducks in a row, no matter at what price, would bring me peace. I had locked up my spirit, I had ravaged my body, all in an attempt to be safe. I didn't know that surrender was the passport to wholeness. In this third dimensional reality, it is easy to forget that we have agreed to experience our karmic lessons. To infuse these lessons with grace and to find the nugget of opportunity is what is necessary to transform the seemingly insurmountable pain into a gracious gift.

In our culture, the illusion of having control is huge. For me, maintaining control of my external world gave me the mistaken notion that I was safe within. The more I was able to accept myself, the easier it was to let go of that control. I was becoming who I was already. My authentic self. Validating myself rather than looking for validation on the outside became a huge energy gain.

Despite my need for control, I had become so accustomed to just getting by. I had become apathetic. My lower chakras were blocked. I had no "roots" into the ground. I felt afraid, unsafe, unbalanced. Like a dark shadow, fear followed me everywhere. Fear of being alone, fear of losing control, and fear of finances. I felt bad about myself, my body, my life. I was not able to birth myself, my mission, my purpose, my life. In a healthy system, fresh ideas and creative thoughts are first conceived, then slowly incubated, and at the appropriate moment, delivered into the world. When our lower chakras are balanced, life force—Creative Intelligence—expresses itself in many ways, one of the most significant being a healthy sexuality.

My sexuality was stagnant. I discovered that Creative Intelligence expresses itself freely through heart-centered and loving sexual connections. A passion for life, passion for your beloved, working with passion, these are all fuels that feed the creative fire. Creative Intelligence is the Source.

Sexuality is meant to be experienced as graceful, loving, awesome, and fun. I became more and more agitated. My life force wanted to be released. Like a combustion engine inside me, it churned, urging me to ground myself, fulfill my purpose, and create the life I knew was mine. Another step to opening my heart, opening my body was about to take place. After a prolonged period of aloneness and voluntary celibacy, I finally met the man I felt sure was my beloved partner. We flew around the heavens for a while. He told me that he was my gift. His fire was able to break through all of my resistance, all of my excuses, my refusal to connect with my body and all of the obstacles that I thought would keep me safe and in control. My heart opened so wide, my body followed. Years of stagnation and reluctance to love were cleared away. He was indeed my gift, though not the gift I had expected him to be. He left when his work was complete.

My own attitudes, perspectives, and sexual behaviors had been misinformed, misused, distorted, and limited. My husband did not welcome a free expression of my sexuality. I misinterpreted that and internalized it as inadequacy. Surely, there was something "wrong" with me. I closed my body and took up permanent residence in my head. Being in touch with our own sexual energy, with or without a partner, is God's greatest gift, a unique opportunity to allow the Creative Intelligence, in its most powerful way, to break down resistance; to unleash its awesome force within us; to dispel the darkness; to awaken to love.

For a while, the ending of the relationship that I thought was the love of my life plummeted me into despair. My old victim consciousness reemerged. How could this happen? Had I not "worked" on myself long enough? Why did I attract a man who could not be with me? The hurt was so deep I thought that I would never recover. Creative Intelligence does not make mistakes. It was I who interpreted this painful chapter as unfair, another blunder. In reality it was yet another opportunity to clear doubt and blame. He had come to be my leading man and show me new dance steps. In truth, he was just the vehicle. It was really Source, Creative Intelligence leading me into my own body, so that the cosmic dance within me could unfold more completely. What you resist will persist. I surrendered. I learned to accept. I let go of my attachment, my perception of how things should be that was causing me so much pain. I took a deeper step in trust and faith.

Our body is the channel, the antenna for attracting. The vibration that we put out is exactly what we attract. The "higher" energies of trust, faith, intuition, and unconditional love vibrate at frequencies starting around 200. Anger, fear, doubt, and similar negative energies vibrate at a lower frequency. I was attracting what I was feeling—more of the same.

I was learning, slowly learning to live with grace, not fear. I was slowly learning to anchor the presence of Creative Intelligence, to process and clear my emotions, to speak clearly when I felt hurt, to set healthy boundaries, to walk my talk. The fountain of youth is the ability to feel Creative Intelligence, even in the face of suffering; to stay current. No need to wait until suffering settles in the body. Everything is conceived in the spiritual dimension first. We become worthy, open, welcoming vessels to ground and birth Creative Intelligence, and ultimately to welcome change, one of the gateways for Creative Intelligence to find expression in the physical. The word becomes flesh.

Another powerful gateway to invite Creative Intelligence to orchestrate our life is through acceptance and surrender. Struggling against what already is makes no sense. I still experience initial inner rebellion, but practicing acceptance and surrender is easier. I now understand that in the world of form, things are not always fine. Circumstances change, collapse, redefine themselves. If I argue with what is, I am not at peace. Peace does not mean to be in a place where there is no noise, trouble, or hard work. It means to be in the midst of those things and still be calm in your heart. Surrender to the divine plan. In all my busyness to control, to be like everyone else, to stay with the program—or rather every one else's program—to keep a perfect home, be a perfect wife, I lost sight, overlooking and ignoring what my intuition was telling me. I surrendered how I thought my life would turn out. I surrendered perceived expectations. I stopped going against the flow. Only then did I experience peace. From now on, no matter how busy my life, no matter what the circumstances, there is just God and me.

I have experienced this God force, this Creative Intelligence, not only as a sacred sexual passion but also as a fire, a purifying fire, that burns, indeed has to burn, the dense accumulation of frozen and unaddressed emotions woven through my body. The dark night of the soul is the wake-up call that there is so much more to life than to just survive. Addictions are just a repetition of old story lines that follow a familiar circuit in the body. I was addicted to suffering. I knew nothing else. Wayne Dyer once said "If you insist on following the herd, you're bound to trample into a lot of bullshit." I didn't want to follow the herd, but I couldn't trust myself to follow my guidance either, so I stagnated. I tried to fit in. I tried to follow the societal "recipe" for success. I lived in a lovely home, drove an expensive car. I had a husband and two dogs. What could possibly be wrong?

I now care enough about myself to protect myself from difficult situations. My body alerts me when an interaction is draining me. I no longer have a need to fix other people. Giving must be from fullness, not from emptiness. I care enough for myself not to hold negative energies toward another. I learned how to protect the quality of energy in my own heart. Did I leave anything unsaid or undone? What do I need to forgive? What do I feel bitter about? My heart now wants to be free to express. I want to see people authentically rather than through the narrow lens of my unfinished business. I choose to feel and release.

To give love is easy. I can still use my measuring stick and "gauge" how much I give. Receiving love still challenges me. It makes me feel more vulnerable. Being able to receive has to be supported by the strong inner validation that I do deserve love, attention, and devotion. I forgive myself for closing my body, my heart to receiving. I forgive all the actors who played their part in the screenplay that I created for my life. Ultimately, forgiveness does not even exist when attention is in the present moment. Maintaining the truth that there is only the now, that there is only present time, makes forgiveness easy because there is nothing to forgive. The past does not exist in this moment. Yesterday does not exist anymore. You're looking at a new person. We all do the best we can with the awareness that we have.

Changing the behavior without redirecting the energy from

within can only bring the smallest reward. True change reaches down to the cellular level and sheds the layers of illusion, the lies that are embodied and mistaken for truth. Anguish is mostly created from within—through incorrect beliefs and misinterpretations. Even now, I notice myself making an assumption, projecting blame or jumping to some quick unexamined conclusion. In each moment that I step out of the wound, the gift is reclaimed. In each moment, awareness illuminates my thinking. Like a healing balm, a gentle breeze, present moment awareness gently shifts and transforms the old landscape. I am renewed.

Change is healthy and inevitable. I now observe when my body tightens in response to an old message that says rigidity means safety. I notice when I get trapped in old thinking. I notice when my memory cells put on their battle gear to fight yet another fruitless war with Creative Intelligence. I now recognize when old habits prompt me to cover up challenges with more mental noise. I feel the discomfort when I get trapped in incessant and involuntary thinking. I now see when I become a slave to the mind. I now recognize when the proverbial monkey on my back (or in my head) tells me I need to figure it out, lay awake at night, worry about some scary, imagined scenario.

When a situation, a relationship, or a circumstance overwhelms me, I stop, breathe, and gently inquire within. Sometimes, what I'm experiencing is a situation that I've put on automatic based on old assumptions and that the universe is nudging me to review. Sometimes, I notice myself going into overload over a misperception, an old message tenaciously embedded in my unconscious. Sometimes, my body screams, "No, don't go there!" Sometimes, I simply don't know. Or rather, I know that I don't know. For sure, too much discomfort, pain, or struggle always lets me know that I'm not aligned. Less struggle, less effort, more peace. As I let go, my body remembers the peace. I relax. I practice what I know and teach.

The headache, my main teacher, has now been completely and totally resolved. It is a memory that has dissolved into the past. Some of my energy drains are restored into energy gains. Some have not. I am still "under construction," but I do intend to master my thoughts, my emotions, and take responsibility for how they impact my physical structure.

Universal law directs Creative Intelligence. Just as with the law of gravity, this is so whether or not you believe in it. We are already whole and complete. We only have to remember. We are hard-wired for God. Sacred truths live within us.

I believe these sacred truths to be: **All is One** in the first chakra; **Honor Each Other** in the second chakra; **Honor Yourself** in the third chakra; **Love is Divine Power** lives in the heart chakra, where we are tutored from within; **Surrender** to the divine plan and speaking your truth is in the throat chakra; **Seeking Truth** and letting go of illusions resonates with the sixth chakra; and finally, the seventh chakra illuminates the importance of **Living in the Present Moment**.

Living and practicing these sacred truths keeps us aligned. The past is released. Attention is in the present. Only by being in the **now**, can I bless and release the past.

Creative Intelligence is *you*. *You* are the peace that surpasses all understanding.

Out of the wound, comes the gift.

"THERE IS NOTHING ABOUT ME THAT YOU CANNOT ATTAIN. I HAVE NOTHING THAT DOES NOT COME FROM GOD. THE DIFFERENCE BETWEEN US NOW IS THAT I HAVE NOTHING ELSE."
~ QUOTED BY JESUS FROM A COURSE IN MIRACLES

About
Lydia Van den Broeck

Lydia Van den Broeck, Ph.D. is an Energy psychologist, an Energy Mastery coach, an intuitive healer, and inspirational speaker with over twenty years of experience both in the United States and in Europe.

Lydia created the Energy Mastery™ coaching model based on the fact that everything at its finest level of creation is energy. She created the model from her personal desire to quickly release blocked energy and reconnect to alignment effortlessly. When blocked energy is released from the mind and body, natural flow is restored and we are able to reconnect with Creative Intelligence. An energy drain then becomes an energy gain. She knows, from personal experience, that this powerful energy then becomes available to manifest and co-create a new way of being.

Energy Mastery Method™ is a unique and powerful way to instantly recalibrate and redirect blocked energy. As an Energy Mastery coach, Lydia uses her innate intuitive abilities to read her client's energy field and help them identify and clear the energies and beliefs that interfere with creating a fulfilling life professionally, personally, emotionally, and spiritually.

Lydia works one-on-one with clients in person or by phone, as well as in groups. Her work includes an energy assessment, clearing energy drains, an energy transmission, and an overall balancing of the chakras. She encourages her clients to continue accessing deeper levels of awareness by weaving sacred principles such as compassion, faith, trust, and integrity into their practical daily experiences.

Lydia also facilitates the Wholeness in the Workplace™ workshops on self-mastery and intuition to increase leadership, productivity, and profits in major corporations, academic institutions, and not-for-profit organizations. An experienced and passionate trainer, she recognizes the need to work with the *whole* person: Mind, Body, and Spirit. Her programs successfully bridge professional development and personal renewal.

Born in Antwerp, Belgium, Lydia came to the United States in 1986, after having lived in London, England for almost twenty years. As a linguist, she was initially teaching foreign languages to executives in major organizations. Lydia earned her Bachelor's degree from the University of London and her Master's and Doctorate degrees in Wholistic Sciences and Psychotherapy from Columbia Pacific University in California. While living in London, she ran a successful hypnotherapy and psychotherapy practice. She has been published in several American and British periodicals and has been a frequent guest on BBC Radio London.

Lydia Van den Broeck, Ph.D. is available for private sessions, corporate and community workshops, and keynotes. To contact Lydia, call 630-792-9020 or email lydia7777@wowway.com or lydia@lydiavandenbroeck.com, or for more information, visit www.lydiavandenbroeck.com.

Life's Choices

___

By Ted Prodromou

Tom woke up early that fateful morning. "Why in the world am I awake at this ungodly hour?" he thought to himself, as he squinted at the 5:15 illuminating the digital clock on his bed stand. As he lay in bed trying to go back to sleep, he noticed light around the edges of his window shades, and the pleasant sound of birds chirping outside. After months of winter and long, dark nights, spring had finally arrived. Tom had a sudden burst of energy and couldn't resist the urge to go for a walk.

Tom hadn't had a desire to go for a walk in years. His normal routine consisted of rolling out of bed after many battles with the snooze alarm, showering, drinking a pot of coffee while eating a greasy breakfast, and heading off to work for another twelve-hour day. However, today, for some reason, he was being pulled to go for a walk before work. His wife, Mary, didn't know what to make of this. In twenty years of marriage, her husband had never jumped out of bed to go for a walk. "Miracles do happen," Mary exclaimed, as Tom bounced joyfully toward the front door.

Dashing out the front door of his suburban ranch-style house, Tom walked through his upscale subdivision outside of San Francisco toward the rising sun. A few minutes later, he reached the open space near his house. As he neared the end of the sidewalk, he noticed a narrow dirt trail winding up a hill. He decided to follow the uneven path and started up the gentle slope. However, the walk became more difficult as he climbed higher. At last, Tom reached the top of the hill, stopping to catch his breath. Huffing and puffing, he looked around. Turning in every direction, he admired the breathtaking views. He could see for miles in every direction. "I had no idea the view was so beautiful from here," he thought to himself. "I've lived in this neighborhood for twenty years and I have never walked up this hill."

Sweaty and tired from his climb, Tom sat down to rest before he headed back down the trail. As he paused, he listened to the sound of birds singing to each other, as others glided effortlessly over his head. He watched his surroundings, as a bright, orange fireball rose quickly from the horizon. The sight mesmerized Tom. "I don't remember the last time I sat and watched the sun rise," he thought. "It's just amazing." Usually, Tom was driving to work while the sun rose and he rarely noticed it, unless it was in his face, blinding him. Instead of noticing its beauty, he would curse it in annoyance.

As the sun continued its journey across the sky, Tom decided to get back on the trail. However, instead of retracing his steps, he chose to go in the other direction. He was curious to see where the trail ended. An overwhelming force was pulling Tom on this magnificent journey and he was enjoying himself immensely. He couldn't wait to see what was next on his journey. "Work can wait a little longer," he said to himself.

The trail led Tom down the backside of the hill, switching back and forth through the trees that were just beginning to spring to life after the long winter. Buds were blossoming, birds were chirping, animals were calling out to each other. The air was refreshing and clear, with the smell of fresh grass and flowers penetrating his senses. There wasn't a cloud in the sky, and the sun began to burn off the morning chill. Tom became more energized with every step, and began to jog down the hill. He hadn't felt this great in years.

Reaching the bottom of the hill, he came to a river and followed the trail along its bank, watching the currents and listening to the rapids. The river flowed through the forest of redwood trees, winding back and forth. The smell changed from fresh grass and flowers to fresh water and forest. With every breath, Tom felt better.

As the trail led him around the bend, Tom saw an abandoned yellow raft on the side of the river. He looked around to see to whom it might belong, but nobody was in sight. He decided to take a ride in the raft. "What the heck, I'll be back in a few minutes," he thought. He jumped in and began rowing with the wooden paddle that had been lying inside the raft.

The river was calm and quiet. Tom paddled easily, taking in the sights, sounds, and smells of Mother Nature. He observed his surroundings. Giant redwood trees climbing endlessly into the sky, bright green ferns growing in the forest, deer wandering along the shores of the river, squirrels scampering along the tree branches, birds soaring above the river looking for breakfast, and fish swimming deep in the river. Nature was out in full force and Tom was enjoying the show.

As he drifted along the lazy river, his mind began to slow down and ideas began to pop into his head. Solutions to his problems appeared out of nowhere. Things that had been on his mind came into focus, with incredible clarity. Each breath he took became slower, richer, and deeper. A deep sense of relaxation overtook his body. His fingers and toes tingled. His backache disappeared. The stress he felt throughout his body melted away. He could drift forever like this, afloat in the moment.

The feeling reminded Tom of his childhood when his grandmother would tell him about listening to his intuition. "Quiet your mind by sitting still and relaxing. Notice the sensations throughout your body, especially in your chest and stomach," she would say. "If you stay very still and concentrate on this feeling, it will guide you through life. When you're troubled, you can ask for help and your intuition will give you subtle signs that will eventually provide the answer for you."

Tom and his siblings loved to sit around the fire on cold, winter evenings, absorbing their grandmother's wisdom. They spent hours together, hearing her stories, practicing stillness, and listening to their inner voices. Grandma would guide them through relaxation exercises to help them connect with their bodies. He remembered using his internal guidance system countless times throughout his early life. Often, when he was stressed in school or at work, he would sit still, relax, and ask for assistance. Always, his intuition provided the guidance he needed to move past the difficult situation. Unfortunately, the stress of his job had made him forget about this wonderful gift Grandma had taught him.

In the distance Tom heard some rumbling. "There must be a storm brewing. It sounds like thunder ahead," he thought. He was so busy thinking about his childhood he didn't think twice about any other possibilities.

Tom continued to drift down the river, enjoying the peacefulness and serenity of the moment. He felt like a child again, playing in the river. He remembered the times he spent vacationing on the Truckee River when he was growing up. He loved canoeing on the river, but there was always an adult with him in the canoe. He had never been alone on the river—until now.

Tom noticed his raft was moving a little faster. The river was getting narrower and the greenish-brown water was beginning to bubble with small whitecaps. The calm, quiet river was beginning to speak louder. "I'm picking up some speed," Tom thought. "This is fun!" He laid back and began hooting and hollering as the raft moved faster through the channel of water.

Suddenly, the river took a sharp turn to the right. Tom couldn't see what was around the bend and couldn't care less. He was a kid again enjoying himself. "I need to spend less time at work and more time enjoying life," Tom said out loud above the rapidly moving water. "This is the best time I've had in years."

As Tom rounded the bend, the river started churning. The serenity and peacefulness suddenly ended. The river was now screaming, roaring louder and louder every second. The water around him was completely white, exploding against the rocks. His raft began to take on water.

Tom sat up and tried to slow the raft. Faster and faster, the river flowed, taking the raft with it. The waves crashed higher, the sound roaring in his ears. He had no control of the raft and started to panic. He screamed for help, but there was no one to help him. He held on, wondering how to stop the craft. He was trapped and totally out of control.

The river kept growing in strength and Tom was in a complete panic. The rapids were now higher than Tom and he was bouncing around like a pinball. As the raft rounded the next bend, he saw the river drop from view. He realized that he was headed toward a large waterfall. He couldn't stop. Tom felt he was about to die. Nobody could help him and he started to pray.

The raft shot over the waterfall, flew into the air, and dropped straight down. He tried to hang on, but the raft slipped away. As he fell through the air, waiting to crash to his death below, his life flashed before his eyes. Memories of his childhood appeared in his mind. Going to school on his first day of kindergarten. Riding his bike around his neighborhood in the summertime. Swimming at his neighbor's pool. His first kiss. His celebrated high school athletic career. Captain of the football, basketball, and track teams. Dating the best looking cheerleader, and then marrying her! The birth of his children. Changing his first diaper. The children's' first steps. These memories and more ran through his mind as he continued to fall.

Suddenly, everything began to move in slow motion. The fall felt incredibly peaceful, like floating on a soft cloud, gently dropping downward. Every passing second seemed like a day. In Tom's mind, he was falling to his death below. Completely helpless, he wondered when he would crash and die. It was not *if* he was going to die, but *when*. "There's no way I can survive this fall," Tom thought to himself. Over and over he flipped as he dropped like a rock, out of control. "This is not how I thought my life would end. I've been such a selfish person," he thought as he continued to drop. "If I only had another chance at life, I would be a different person."

His memories continued to move through his mind. Tom had become desensitized to life and his intuition over the years. Long commutes and workdays, stress, poor eating habits, and sleepless nights had taken their toll on him. Work was difficult, with layoffs and cutbacks resulting in less people doing more work. Morale was horrible. People came to work each day wondering if they were the next department to be outsourced.

Life at home was worse. Tom and Mary rarely spoke to each other. They both worked stressful jobs and were completely exhausted at the end of the day. They lived separate lives in the same house. It seemed that the only thing they had in common was their children, Ryan and Chelsea. They were dropped off at school in the morning and weren't picked up until 6:30 at night. Tom was rarely involved in shuttling the kids to and from school because he left for work early and came home very late most nights. It was no surprise that both kids were starting to act up in school.

Tom had been so caught up in his daily routine he didn't realize he was in such a miserable trap until he had started drifting down the river. His life was all work and no play. He was withdrawing into a shell, isolating himself from his family and friends.

He had lost the connection with his inner voice, that Creative Intelligence that helped to gently guide him on the journey. It had been ignored for so long, it was now screaming at him to wake up and notice what his life had become. The signs of discontent and unhappiness had been there for years, but Tom kept brushing them away, choosing to focus on his work instead. He had ignored that inner voice out of fear.

He knew his relationship with Mary and the kids was superficial, but knowing separation or divorce was a distinct possibility, he didn't want to be alone. To avoid the inevitable, he worked longer hours.

But at work he was going through the motions because his job was unfulfilling and routine. There was an endless amount to do and he'd never catch up, no matter how many hours he worked. He once loved going to his job, but now he could care less. He had no passion for his work. There was no fire left in him. He just kept running from the truth that his relationship with his family was failing, and work, his secret hiding place, held no joy.

Suddenly, Tom's body smacked the water in the lagoon. The deep, loud thud was barely heard because of the thunderous sound of the waterfall. Tom's body floated motionless, face down in the water. He drifted through the lagoon and down the river, bouncing off rocks, as his lifeless body began picking up speed.

As the river continued its relentless journey with its new companion, a fisherman on the riverbank noticed Tom's limp body floating down the river. The man quickly jumped up and yelled to Tom. He started following the lifeless form down the river, trying desperately to reach him. Tom continued to bob up and down in the river, still bouncing off the rocks. The fisherman ran down the river ahead of Tom and climbed out on a large rock in the river. He reached out and tried to snag Tom's body, but came up short. He ran further down the river, yelling frantically for help.

Finally, the fisherman's friends heard his pleas for help. They joined him in the rescue effort, scrambling toward the river. "What should we do?" one of the men screamed. "Let's run down the river past the next bend," yelled the fisherman. "There's a large branch hanging across the river."

As the entire group ran down the river, the first man climbed out on the branch. The river was rushing below and the limb began to sag as he inched his way out above the river's rushing current. He was shaking with fear, but he kept moving further out on the branch. His heart was pounding like a huge drum in his chest. He was scared to death, but he kept crawling. He could almost reach Tom as he drifted down the river. The branch was bowing and the fisherman was shaking violently, but he continued to move.

Tom was approaching fast, so the fisherman had to act quickly. He stretched out completely on the branch, wrapping his legs at tight as he could. His face and hands were dripping with sweat. He wondered if he could hang on and still grab Tom as he drifted by. Tom went underwater a few feet before he reached the branch. The fisherman stretched as far as he could and reached down toward the water. Suddenly, Tom's body popped out of the water right into the man's outstretched hands. He grabbed Tom with all his strength. He was holding on for dear life, clenching Tom's heavy, waterlogged body. "I got him," he yelled.

The fisherman was trying as hard as he could to hold onto Tom, but he couldn't move. Tom's weight and the flow of the current pushed his lifeless body into the branch, bending it so far that it was touching the water. They were now both trapped. To get up, the fisherman would have to let go of Tom. Every muscle in his body was screaming with pain.

At that moment, Tom began to wake from his unconscious state. His eyes opened slowly and he wondered where he was and why a complete stranger hanging from a tree branch was in the middle of a rushing river holding him. Meanwhile, his rescuer struggled to hang on. Tom started to grab onto the tree branch to pull himself out of the water. "CRAAACK!" The branch snapped and fell into the water with both men hanging on. They floated down the river holding onto each other.

Working their way to the side of the river, they swam into a small inlet. Both men were completely exhausted as they crawled onto the shore. The other men came running to help them. The rescuer was bleeding, and Tom was seriously bruised and his left leg was shattered. But he was alive.

Shivering and in a state of shock, Tom laid on the bank of the river. The man who had saved him sat next to him. The bleeding was under control, but his chest was full of cuts and scrapes from the tree branch. The other men moved to care for both of them. They couldn't believe both men survived the ordeal, especially Tom. After seeing his unconscious body floating down the river, they were amazed to see him still alive.

Tom's recovery was slow and painful. His body was damaged from head to toe. In addition to his broken leg, many ribs were cracked. Dark bruises covered his body. Tom spent the next month in the hospital recovering from his injuries. The physical recovery took months. His emotional recovery took even longer.

Lying in the hospital bed gave Tom plenty of time to reflect on his life. He felt every emotion: sadness, guilt, anger, rage, insecurity, love, and hate, and soon fell into a depression.

"I've been wasting my life and neglecting my family," he thought to himself. "I've ignored my wife and children; I'm selfish; I only care about work; I'm not doing a good enough job at work; I have no friends; I'm all alone . . ." and on and on his gremlins shouted. Tom felt like he had wasted the past twenty years of his life.

If only Tom had listened to that voice of knowing, that Creative Intelligence. It had always been there, sending him signals to change the path he was on, but he had chosen to ignore its subtle signs. If only he had paid attention!

Tom had allowed fear to overwhelm and paralyze him. Instead of addressing his issues, he had made up stories to justify his actions. Fear told him that his relationship with Mary and the kids wasn't that bad. Fear told him that his blood pressure wasn't that high. Fear told him that his weight wasn't out of control.

Late one night as he battled insomnia, Tom saw an infomercial by Tony Robbins. He had seen this one before and hadn't cared for it. There were a number of people in a focus group talking about their lives. Most were unhappy and unsatisfied, but had no idea what to do about it. They didn't think they could change and actually be happy. They were trapped in a life made up of long work days, long commutes in bumper-to-bumper traffic, and earning just enough to pay their monthly bills. They were overweight and unhealthy. Tom related to this focus group. "They're in the same boat I am!"

Tony Robbins then entered the room and began asking the focus group questions. "How do you feel every morning when you have to get up?" he asked.

"Terrible," most people answered.

"I feel sick to my stomach every morning," one woman exclaimed.

"What's your body telling you?" Tony asked. "Are you listening to your inner voice or are you blocking it out?"

"Obviously I'm blocking it out," she said.

"Do you know that you have choice?" Tony asked. "You can choose to be happy and successful in life or you can choose to be miserable and unhappy," he explained.

"Every morning when you wake up, do you choose to be happy or unhappy?" he asked. "Is your intuition telling you to change something in your life? It's never too late to make changes in your life," he told the group. "Beginning tomorrow, before you get out of bed, make a conscious choice to be happy and successful. Listen carefully to your intuition, and trust the message it's sending you. Tell yourself that, 'Today is going to be the best day of my life.' "

Tom was intrigued by this simple suggestion. "What do I have to lose?" he thought. "I'm not waiting until tomorrow morning. I choose to be happy starting right now." He began remembering what it was like when he was young and happy. Tom visualized himself as a kid again playing with his friends, without a worry in the world. It felt really good. He could feel it in his body. Happy, relaxed, having fun, with no worries at all.

Tom continued to think about being happy and successful. "What will make me happy today?" he thought. Tom had enjoyed playing with his children when they were young. He would take them to the park and they would play for hours in the playground. "What can I do with the kids tomorrow?" he thought. "What can Mary and I do together that would be fun ?" Tom now had a huge smile on his face and a calm feeling ran through his body. He soon drifted off into a deeper sleep than he'd had in years.

When Tom woke up the next morning, his mind was racing. "Today, I choose to be happy and successful," he repeated to himself. He saw himself being successful at work and even more successful at home with his family. He saw himself making more money than ever and loving work again. He saw himself being closer than ever to Mary and spending quality time with both kids. He attended their music events at school, drove on school field trips, and actually started coaching their sports teams. He was the model father and husband. Tom continued to visualize his perfect life. "I am happy and successful," he repeated. "I listen to my intuition and trust the messages every day," he added.

After a half-hour of this meditation and visualization, Tom got out of bed and announced, "I choose to be happy and successful today!" He went downstairs and cooked a wonderful pancake breakfast complete with bacon and fresh fruit for his family. Mary and the kids were pleasantly surprised when they came downstairs and found Tom in his chef's apron cooking away. He was happy and cheerful for the first time in years. They didn't know what had happened overnight to create this amazing transformation and wondered how someone could change so much in a matter of hours.

"Tom, what happened to you last night?" Mary asked. "You are a completely different person today. I love the new you."

"Well, Mary, I was watching this crazy infomercial late last night and I discovered a simple but amazing secret," Tom rejoiced. "I learned that I can make a choice every day. I can choose to be happy or I can choose to be sad every minute of every day. Today, I've chosen to be happy. What do you think?"

"I think it's amazing, Tom. But is it really that simple? Can I really choose to be happy every day if I want?"

"So far so good for me. I haven't felt this great in years."

From that day on, Tom made a conscious choice every morning to be happy and to listen to his intuition. He chose to focus on the positives in his life. He chose to spend at least 30 minutes a day meditating or relaxing so he could stay in touch with his intuition. The result was truly amazing. Everyone at work and all of Tom's friends were astonished at how much he changed in such a short time. Everything in his life was getting better each day.

Tom began to stay at home later in the morning to drop the kids off at school on his way to work. He made it home each night for dinner and he never missed any of his children's school events. He loved driving on the class field trips and was usually the only father. His relationship with Mary was better than ever. Mary also made a conscious choice to be happy every morning and they were like newlyweds again. Tom became the model father and husband he had visualized that first morning, and was loving life again.

He became so confident in his abilities that he chose to leave his unfulfilling job and became a leadership and management consultant. He started writing articles and books and he became one of the most sought after speakers in the country. He was often seen on daytime talk shows, including Oprah, Today, Good Morning America, CNBC, and CNN, where he became the host of his own show called Leadership in America. He commanded thousands of dollars for each speech and consulted with only the "best of the best" executives.

Tom's dramatic life changes also impacted Mary and the kids. Mary chose a different path in life. Her new-found confidence allowed her to quit her job and start working with underprivileged children. She opened a children's center that included homework labs, tutoring, free classes, and computers. Her dream of helping the less fortunate became reality.

The children also excelled. Both children volunteered daily at the children's center, helping students with their homework and leading many of the after school games. Both Ryan and Chelsea finished near the top of their graduating class. After finishing college, they came back to work with Mary, helping her expand the community center to neighboring towns.

Tom's former lifestyle is, unfortunately, very typical in our fast-paced world. People get caught up in routines and time flies by. Most of us spend our days reacting to what life throws at us instead of living the life of our dreams. Our intuition, our Creative Intelligence, is constantly sending us messages, but most of the time we're too busy to stop and listen.

Life is like Tom's river. Sometimes the flow is slow and easy, at other times it can turn you upside down. Sometimes you move forward, sometimes backward, sometimes sideways and sometimes you get stuck in one place. You never know what's around the next bend. If you ever get too comfortable, you can bet that life will throw some rapids into your path.

But your intuition is your secret weapon that will help you through the ups and downs of life. If you slow down and listen to what your body is telling you, it will let you know that something is changing. Your intuition provides insight and guidance. The secret is to stop, feel it, and trust the message you receive, especially when it's a stressful situation. Your Creative Intelligence will guide you to a life in which you live life on your terms, instead of reacting to life's emergencies.

Make conscious choices every day. Choose to be happy, choose to be sad, choose to be successful—choose to be whatever you want to be. When you make a conscious choice, you are in complete control of your feelings and emotions. Allow Creative Intelligence to help you navigate life's rough water. When you make that choice, you will always reach your destination.

About
Ted Prodromou

Ted Prodromou, CPCC, worked in the Information Technology field for over 20 years before becoming a personal coach in 2001. Ted worked for IBM, Digital Equipment Corporation, Cellular One, and Putnam Lovell Securities before starting his own computer consulting company, Valiss IT, seven years ago. Despite a thriving consulting practice, spending most of his day with computers and computer networks began to get old. Missing the interaction with people, he became a Certified Personal Co-Active Coach (CPCC) in 2001, and started a personal coaching practice in addition to his computer consulting practice. He now coaches individuals through career transitions, and leads workshops throughout the U.S. and Canada.

Today, Ted is living his dream life, working from home, running two successful businesses while coaching his children's sports teams. He's actively involved in his community, serving on the local school district's technology committee, and is a board member for the Yes Foundation, which raises money for local schools.

Ted is a graduate of the Co-Active Space Leadership program, as well as the Steven Covey Masters Coaching Program. Ted is also a member of the International Coach Federation (ICF) and a certified facilitator for Speaking Circles International, a transformational speaking program.

.

What Do You See?
Re-Creating Your Life
Through the Eyes of a Child

By Deborah Gordon Bernstein

"THERE IS NO GREATER INSPIRATION THAN THAT OF A CHILD DISCOVERING THE WONDERS OF THE WORLD." ~ DEBORAH GORDON BERNSTEIN

My Inspiration

The day was gray, with clouds threatening to open into a downpour at any moment. My two-year-old daughter, Sarah, and I were walking to her grandparent's house for dinner, a two-minute walk. From my perspective as a good mother, I tried to hurry us along to beat the rain. Sarah, however, did not seem to feel the same impending doom or need to rush. As we meandered along, she looked into the gray sky and with great excitement said, "Mommy, look. There are two birds!" I had seen the birds above through my peripheral vision, but paid no particular attention, as I see birds all the time this way. My daughter stopped, looked up again, pointed, and adamantly said, "Mommy, stop. Look at the birds!" So I stopped and really looked at them for a few moments. I noticed how very large they were, extraordinarily high in the sky. And I noticed how incredibly graceful they were. I wondered what it would be like to fly freely, and marveled at the amazing feat. I also thought that it must be an awesome perspective of the world from that incredible height.

Sarah stopped again. "Mommy, look at those silly trees." I looked to where she was pointing and saw six huge, beautiful spruces swaying back and forth in the wind. They seemed almost to their breaking point. Again, as I really saw those trees I thought how amazing it was that with the very strong gusts they just go with the flow and do not break; definitely a lesson to be learned there. This struck me as a metaphor for the flow of life.

The next thing I noticed was Sarah giggling, the way only a toddler can that lights up your world. I asked what was so funny? "The wind tickles my nose." I stopped and felt the wind too, and it was a very funny sensation to really notice and feel the warm wind wash over me. We continued our walk and Sarah stopped, noticing every pebble, piece of grass, flower, branch, and squirrel. She noticed the cracks in the road. "The sidewalks are as high as mountains," she exclaimed, and one mailbox looked like clouds. She noticed green grass and brown grass and beautiful, yellow buttercup flowers, all things that I would not have given a second thought to, but because of her, stopped to really look, notice, and appreciate. I saw the world through her eyes, and found her view to be interesting and fascinating, in fact, amazing. I felt happier, more relaxed and playful, in awe of the simple wonders of nature. Our two-minute walk turned into a fifteen-minute adventure and just as we reached Grandma's house the rain began to fall. "Mommy I'm getting wet," she laughed as she ran to the door.

It's All About Perspectives

I realized Sarah was demonstrating one of the concepts I use in coaching—choosing perspectives. I cannot change the facts of the situation, but I can help a client change their view of those facts, which in turn changes their choices, ultimately resulting in a change in their quality of life. On the day we walked to Grandma's house the facts were that it was gray, with birds flying, and trees swaying. I was in the perspective of let's hurry before the rain, and she was in the perspective of noticing with amazement everything around her while having an adventure. We each had a choice about how to interpret the facts and how to experience them. Now really, what would happen if we got caught in the rain? As sweet as Sarah is, I know neither she nor I would melt. It would just be another funny story.

That journey inspired me to write this message: Life is about perspectives—what we choose to see and how we choose to experience living and thus create our life.

The other day I noticed Sarah jumping and skipping and I asked why she always did this. She said, "Mommy, I am just so excited." I asked what she was excited about. "I don't know. Just everything!"

"Wow!" I thought. "What a wonderful perspective just to be excited about life. I want some of that." So I tried on that perspective and attitude for a day. Instead of chores and deadlines, I lived in the perspective that everything was exciting.

Simply by being who she is, Sarah helped me crystallize my message and inspired me to write about it, as she is my model for playing with perspectives and making choices about how to live. She demonstrates that every moment reflects what we choose to see. I realized through her that a person can change by asking these powerful questions:

- What do you choose to see when you look at your life or a particular situation?
- What else can you see?
- What do you want to see?
- What would a young, innocent child see?

Another powerful example of choosing perspectives took place recently as I was getting ready for work. Sarah watched as I did my hair, put my makeup on, etc. That particular day, I was thinking how terrible I looked. My daughter, seeing my reflection in the mirror, announced, "I see two beautiful mommies." She kissed the mommy in the mirror and then me. Again, life is about perspectives. She saw two beautiful mommies, while my perception of my reflection was quite the opposite.

I get to choose what I see in the mirror. I paused and asked myself, "What do I see? What do I choose to see? What do I want to see?" What do you see when you look at your reflection?

You can create your life out of limitless possibilities. You can choose to empower yourself, or to be a victim. You can continue to feel powerless, or you can access your inner child, your inner innocence, your inner creativity, freeing you to see more possibilities instead of only the obstacles and the reasons you cannot do something.

Pink Boots

I use the same curiosity that my daughter displays in her expansive world to help clients better understand the affect of their choices on their inner and outer world. I ask my clients to try on different perspectives for a specific period of time to make an informed decision and learn more about themselves. There is no rule that one must forever stay in a chosen perspective, and I encourage clients to try on many points of view. We brainstorm about an issue and then choose one perspective to live in for a period of time. I believe that the more experimentation and the more self-discovery the better.

One day as I was working with my own coach on the topic of building my business, I identified six possible perspectives, settling on one. During the session, I had been walking around the house looking out the windows. I saw my daughter walking with the nanny after a rainfall… in her pink rain boots. She was splashing in puddles, big and small, laughing and giggling. The nanny seemed to be having just as much fun. In fact, they were both laughing so much I wanted to run out and jump in puddles with them, which led me to the perspective I wanted to try on for my business: Pink Boots.

To me, pink signifies lightness, femininity, and playfulness. Splashing in puddles is a metaphor for finding my way as I explore different avenues and build my business. There are so many opportunities, paths to explore, and ways to go about building a practice that ironically I was feeling overwhelmed and disempowered. I realized I just needed to splash in the puddles. I had the perspective that some puddles would take me by surprise, make a big splash, and be beneficial, fun, and rewarding, and jumping in some puddles would have no effect. This new perspective was freeing and playful, and helped me find my way and my niche with less stress. The process was experimental and fun versus feeling like a "job."

After seventeen years of working in the corporate environment, I wanted a significant change. I wanted to work from my authentic self, follow my passions, pursue my aspirations, and realize my dreams. What better place to start than splashing in puddles with curiosity and without attachment to the outcome? Simultaneously, I did this while believing in myself and listening to my inner voice—my Creative Intelligence. It worked. I do not want to mislead you to say that this was not scary and that I had no self doubt. I had reservations and fears. But I tried on this perspective for two weeks, and now frequently revisit it. This new point of view works, and I am learning more about myself and what I want to do, what I am willing to do, and what I am not willing to do to live an authentic and fulfilling life. Pink Boots... I love them.

A Life of Authenticity

Sarah also lets me know when it is time to, as she says, "Pay attention of me now," as she drags me out of my office or off the phone. She cannot tell time yet. However, she senses when it is time for Mommy to stop working. How wonderful to be completely truthful with yourself and others. How wonderful to be in touch with your emotions to know what you need and want, and to ask for it. As adults how many of you have lost the ability to do this? How many times do you say, "I do not even know what I want anymore?"

Ask yourself these questions:
- What do you need most in your life right now?
- What do you need to do to take care of yourself?
- What is missing in your life?
- What is the most important request you have of yourself to improve your quality of life?
- What is the most important request you have for those around you?
- Have you asked for what you need? Why not?
- What will you do to take care of yourself if you do not have your requests met?
- What do you have to lose? What do you have to gain?

Lessons and Wisdom From A Child

Have you ever gone for a walk or to the zoo or a garden or a store with a two year-old? The simplest activities can turn into exciting adventures filled with curiosity and discovery, blended with truthfulness, innocence, joy, and being fully present in the moment. What would it be like to live your life from the view of a young child? Not *as* a young child, but with their essence. How much more exciting, interesting, and adventurous would everything be, even if nothing changed except your perspective? What about trying something new, just to see what happens, without analyzing it first? Have you tried simply jumping into an activity with excitement and curiosity just to see what you would notice and learn?

The beauty in children is that they believe they can do and be anything. This is a wonderful gift. Unfortunately, as we mature we lose sight of possibilities, and thus different opportunities.

How much can you learn from a child? You can learn the joy of simple every day occurrences. You can learn about curiosity, getting out of your comfort zone, and loving unconditionally. What would it be like to feel your emotions when you have them instead of stuffing them and letting them come out somewhere else? What would it be like to laugh, cry, feel the whole range of emotions, and then move on? Recapture that wonderful, joyful, experimental, curious, unconditional, loving essence. The world is an intriguing, exciting place with so much to enjoy.

What is Creative Intelligence?

Creative Intelligence is your ability to create in the moment and to realize that everything you do is forming your life. The key is to allow the natural flow of your creativity to happen so that your essence emerges, allowing your life's purpose and passion to flow with ease. Because you actually create the illusion you call your life, you have the power and the choice to create whatever you want. The choice is yours. What life have you created? Do you want your choice? What do you choose to see? What do you choose for your life?

Creative Intelligence is living life from the flow of your inner knowing before you are socialized with "shoulds," cultural lenses, biases, expectations, aspirations, fears, and insecurities. Creative Intelligence is being your innocent, true, and natural self. It is experimenting and finding what works for you, getting in touch with and living from the place of your authentic self, not from the place of the many facades that develop as you mature and become socialized.

As you grow older, you have the gift not only of creativity, but of experience, wisdom, and intellect. The challenge becomes how to balance all of these gifts so that you continue to allow your life's essence to flow, and simultaneously continue to live in the moment. The alternative is to leave your childlike essence behind and live only in your intellect with the lessons of maturity. When you do that, your aliveness and life's richness begin to diminish. The challenge then becomes how to regain your innate creativity.

Creating Possibilities and Making Deliberate Choices

If you do not create what you want, I guarantee you someone else will create your life for you. You are whole, creative, resourceful, and powerful and from this place you can create a rich and fulfilling life. Remember, all of these things are inherently yours. If you do not have them, you have consciously or probably unconsciously chosen to give them away. You are the only one who can reclaim them.

Others are more than happy to keep them from you, not because they have bad intentions, or even realize what they are doing. They may think that, in fact, they are protecting you. Remember, it is easy to blame others, but it is you who gave away yourself. Others can not take unless you allow them to do so. Sometimes it is easier to let others run your life than take the responsibility. However, reclaiming responsibility is well worth the journey and the challenges inherent in it. Reclaiming this part of your self can be made easier by getting support from a life coach.

You may be asking, "Okay, this sounds great, so how do I do this?" When you are in a situation you do not like, first realize that you are in a perspective. For example, "My job stinks. My boss is a jerk, this job is beneath me. People do not realize what I am capable of. This organization is screwed up, but I need to stay here, where else will I go?" This example is wrought with perspectives, but for illustrative purposes I will take just one because we can only work with one thing at a time. Let us say the issue is *dissatisfaction with the job* and the current perspective is, *"I'm stuck here, I have no choice due to my circumstances."* As a coach, I would ask, "So what does this perspective feel like? What is the benefit of this perspective? What do you gain from the perspective?" Choosing to stay in your perspective may keep you in your comfort zone of not getting what you want, reinforcing low self- esteem, fear of the unknown, fear of risks, etc. So what do you gain and what are the costs? Now let's play with other perspectives: an opportunity to prove myself; opportunity to pursue other interests in life; opportunity to get involved with interesting side projects; a challenge to get a new job; and on and on.

As we explore each perspective, I ask the same questions: What does it really feel like to be in this perspective? What does it look like? What is available to you here? What is the inner and outer energy like? What are the costs?

After we explore each perspective fully, I ask the client to choose one to "try on" for an agreed upon time and we discuss what that looks like. Inevitably, the client comes back with new learning and insights about themselves and about life. The client may or may not like that perspective—and that's fine. They can try on a new one or brainstorm more or combine a few. There is no right answer. The point is inner exploration, finding your stride, finding your true self, and being in alignment with your values and how you truly and deeply want to live. When you are in alignment with your values and vision, you are happy and fulfilled, and when you are not in alignment, you are stressed, unhappy, and disgruntled. Where are you? What do you see? What do you choose?

I truly believe this because I myself am on this journey. I believe it is a deliberate, conscious, and lifelong journey. It is not a destination. I have found the journey to be self-empowering, fulfilling, satisfying, and yes, at times, challenging, scary, and overwhelming. But all in all, it is a place of aliveness and a place where my authentic self can live with full integrity. Going back to your childhood knowing, essence, and curiosity will lead to a more fulfilling life, one that is on purpose and lived with passion, one where you will not have to face the question of, "What if I had chosen...?"

My Journey

There were several pivotal times in my life when I took a good look at where I was in my career and how it aligned with my dreams, goals, and intentions. Eventually, I realized I was on a successful track that no longer truly aligned with my aspirations. I saw that although it was a very lucrative career, it was no longer what I wanted. Many people thought I was crazy, but my passions and personal vision had evolved and I wanted a career that I was again passionate about. I did not want to be at my retirement party with regrets and lack of enthusiasm, and feeling relief that it was finally over. I realize there are times in life when you must take a job to survive and pay the bills. However, I made a conscious decision to get back on the path to my dreams. That decision was not easy. Changing my path took self-awareness first, and then planning, courage, belief in myself, strategizing, support, political savvy, mentoring, and timing. But I got there. I never lost sight of the big picture. This is my life and my dream, passion, and aspiration. In the process of making a new choice, I became reenergized, excited, challenged, and felt like I was living life more fully. I was again living on purpose and tapping into my inner essence.

Contrary to others' view of my career, the truth was my career goals had changed and my inner voice was telling me the time to change was now. If I did not pursue my twenty year-old dream now, then when? I did a lot of soul searching, and realized what I wanted for myself is what I wish for Sarah. My wish for her is that if she wants something, to pursue it whole-heartedly and with full confidence that she can achieve whatever she desires. I want her to fully go after her passions and dreams. To be a role model then,

I must do the same thing and fully pursue my dreams.

In addition, I felt I had lost some of myself and wanted to reconnect with my true essence and pursue my dreams again—a dream, I might add, that I was afraid would always be a dream, leaving me with regrets. I wanted some of that curiosity, innocence, and aliveness back. I wanted to feel lighter and happier. I thought there was a better way to lead my life and raise my daughter.

I am very thankful and grateful for my corporate experience. It was the right thing at the right time. I feel it all led to this moment, now. I learned so much in that experience that actually enabled me to go off on my own. But I had no safety net and it was scary, at times even paralyzing. At times I even thought, "What have I done? Am I crazy? I have a family to support. I am a mother for the first time. Do I need all of this stress?"

Believe it or not, even though I have an MBA, I did not have a business plan. I did not do a market study or any of those other things one is "supposed" to do. I did not really have a contingency plan. I very simply decided to follow my heart, my passion, and my vision and take a leap of faith. I knew what I wanted to do. I just needed to start. Movement and action were the answer.

Before I knew it, doors started to open and things started to happen. I felt a wonderful sense of self-empowerment, as well as a renewed belief in others. The experience was magnificent, astonishing, and energizing, and of course, it continues to evolve to this day. I do not know where the journey will take me and quite honestly I am more interested in the journey than the destination, which is a monumental change in perspective for me. I have never felt anything quite like it before. I am now a full believer that if you put your intentions out to the universe and use your intellect, savvy, and inner knowing, things happen and they work out.

Create the Life That You Want!

Only you can create the life that you want. However, if you do not do this, others will be more than happy to create for you the life *they* want you to have. Embrace everything that happens to you and all of your emotions. Learn from your experiences and create out of the belief of infinite possibilities instead of out of circumstances and limitations. Play with and look for different perspectives. Life is about choices; you do not have to be a victim of your circumstances. That is a choice. Embrace all that you are, trust yourself, and move forward from that place.

Of course, remember that while you are busy making plans for the future, you are in the process of your life, so be in the moment and savor everything that the moment has to offer. Learn from all of your experiences, as this is how you transform yourself. You currently have the power and the resources to create the life you want. Believe that it will happen and this will propel you forward to make it so. Movement is the answer.

Find and reconnect with your inner voice and listen to it. Then take action. It will guide you to your passion, purpose, and a more satisfying, empowering, and fulfilling life.

The Ultimate Question

Get in touch with your essence. From your essence, play with and explore different perspectives. Be creative. This will create infinite choices and possibilities. Choose what you want and consciously and deliberately live the life you choose.

I wish for you that you will re-discover the world from new perspectives and tap into your inner knowing, innocence, and Creative Intelligence so that you can flow with the natural ease of your life, purpose, and passion. And so, I conclude with one question. When you look at your life, "What do you see?"

About
Deborah Gordon Bernstein

Deborah Gordon Bernstein is an adamant believer in life-long learning and personal development. She is a highly skilled and dynamic Leadership Consultant, Executive Coach, Life Coach, Speaker, and Author.

Deborah is the founder and President of DGB Consulting & Coaching Ltd. DGB approaches coaching from a whole person perspective, and therefore, it is common to address both professional and personal challenges throughout the coaching relationship. Through a process of guided self-discovery, clients identify goals and implement actions that bring fulfillment, balance, results, and a true sense of purpose to life. When entering into a coaching relationship with DGB, clients expect to be engaged in new ideas, challenge the status quo, and develop alternative ways to approach important issues. With commitment and intention clients experience on-going success. Clients have said:

"Through my work with Deborah I discovered what was truly holding me back. I am now redesigning my life to be what I want. I learned perspectives are really choices. I found that coaching has a rippling effect. As I have made changes in my life, it has positively impacted the quality of life for my whole family."

"Deborah is an intelligent, insightful, powerful woman who creates a safe environment for me to explore and clarify my goals. She has helped me to move into action toward achieving my vision."

"Wow! After developing a life purpose statement, I felt incredibly powerful. I have never felt anything this powerful or long-lasting in my life. I now know what I want and therefore am making better choices. What an experience!"

DGB's clientele are professional men and women who work either in large corporations or who operate their own business, and also individuals trying to discover their passion and purpose. DGB serves individuals seeking to improve their quality of life to overcome life's obstacles, and achieve their dreams. A sample of DGB's corporate clients include: General Electric, Deloitte, Verizon, Morgan Stanley, DuPont, Time Warner, MasterCard, etc.

Prior to establishing DGB Consulting and Coaching Ltd., Deborah had over seventeen years of in-house corporate experience. Deborah spent ten years at GE, with the last few years of her tenure at Crotonville, GE's Leadership Institute, where she designed, managed, and executed global leadership programs for high potential executives. In this capacity, she worked directly with Jack Welch and his senior leadership team.

DGB Consulting & Coaching Ltd. provides expertise in:
- Leadership Development
- Team Development
- Organization Effectiveness
- Emotional Intelligence
- Executive Coaching
- Life Coaching

DGB services include coaching, consulting, seminars, workshops and speaking services and are offered domestically and globally to individuals and organizations.

Deborah's academic background includes:
- MBA Organizational Behavior, University of Connecticut
- MSW completed coursework, Columbia University
- BA Sociology, cum laude, Brandeis University
- Certified Professional Co-Active Coach, The Coaches Training Institute
- Certified in A Different Kind of Smart™—Applying Emotional Intelligence at Work

To contact DGB, email Deborah@dgb-consulting.com or call 203-847-1580. For more information please visit our website at www.dgb-consulting.com.

Your Map to Creative Intelligence

By Nova Reed

The Island

Imagine a deserted tropical island filled with jungles, peaceful wildlife, and lined with beautiful beaches. This island world exists for enjoyment and fantasy, a remote paradise, a sanctuary of creativity and relaxation. A place where one can refresh their soul, renew their senses, and regain clarity of thought.

Now imagine yourself stranded and completely alone on this deserted island. Years pass, and yet you remain on the island. Your emotional state quickly redefines your island paradise. Boredom, survival in the elements, fear, and loneliness hinder any thoughts of creating a way off the island. Quietly walking the shore no longer holds pleasure. You no longer notice the warm, soft sand beneath your feet, or the natural architectural forms of the coast. Confined by the edges of the island, hopelessness settles in and happiness drifts away across the currents of the ocean. Your existence becomes defined only by your efforts to survive.

Many individuals move through life as if they were stranded on an island, isolated and frustrated with their lack of self-expression and inability to generate creative solutions. They find themselves feeling stuck or trapped within a problem or situation, unable to create. When they are unable to see any solutions to problems with work, home, or life, they have disconnected with their energy of creation.

Creation brings into existence ideas, inventions, beautiful art, literary wonders, and *life*. You were created from two cells, merging together and systematically following multiple stages of differentiation until there is life. As you were created, you were given the molecular fabric of life of which you can further create.

Simply stated, you are born to uniquely express your creative self. Look at any child whose ideals and imaginative self have not been broken, and you will see this spark, this life-giving energy as they play pretend, making believe they are anything at all.

But little by little, the inner voice of your creative self gets stifled by the ideas of others imposing viewpoints that speak of conformity and safety. Creating unique ideas becomes a risk of expression that others may criticize, and you quietly, unknowingly lose your connection with your soulful self to fear. Symptoms of this lack of connection creep into adulthood as general discouragement, lack of joy, and isolation. Others will sense this discontentment as a lack of strength and circle like sharks to further impose their will. At this point, you may experience burn out, turn to self-medication, or remain in a cycle of misguided misery.

But think of the island for a moment. The encircling shoreline is surrounded by water, yes, but change remains constant. With each pounding against the rim of the island, the ocean's tide pushes and pulls layers of sand, changing the shoreline with every lap of water. This is the flow of life. No matter what your emotional state, the flow of life, the energy of creation continually moves to you and offers you the ability to change, to make choices, and to be rescued. The power of creativity exists within all of us, and can be refined and executed using the skill of Creative Intelligence. You can effectively use Creative Intelligence to solve problems, generate positive solutions, and create an abundant life filled with trust, contentment, and fulfillment. You can choose to live on a deserted island—or create your own paradise.

"CREATIVITY CAN SOLVE ALMOST ANY PROBLEM. THE CREATIVE ACT, THE DEFEAT OF HABIT BY ORIGINALITY, OVERCOMES EVERYTHING."
~ GEORGE LOIS

Finding Your Map to Creative Intelligence

On your secluded island, the glowing sun continues to rise each day through the mist of the ocean fog. Breaking the horizon with immeasurable colors refracting and bouncing upon the water, the new light brings a golden glow of hope across the shoreline, waking the sleeping gulls and warming the sand beneath your feet. The constant of the sun reminds you that God will bring you a new day, a new beginning with unspoken possibilities.

There at the shore, where the flow of life and God's will collide, lays your map, resting in a glass bottle. The bottle has no lid or cork laid into it, and yet the map has been protected from the spray of the sea. Upon carefully pulling out the rolled paper, the parchment unravels completely as if it were never coiled.

The parchment is a beautiful golden color, solid and sturdy. The weight of the map feels comfortable and strong. Filters of light seep through the grains of paper emphasizing its age and antiquity. This is the fabric of life. We all have a piece of it given to us by our Creator. Upon it lie beautiful markings drawn with creativity and decisiveness, reflecting years of life, ancient energy, and wisdom. The destinations on the map indicate critical connections you need to fulfill by expressing your creative self. The journey appears long and strenuous, but can take place in an instant. Surely if you follow the map, an abundant treasure will be discovered.

"FOR WHERE YOUR TREASURE IS, THERE WILL YOUR HEART BE ALSO."
~ JESUS CHRIST, MATTHEW 6:21

Your Pack: Self-knowledge

Before you can begin any journey, you need supplies and a way to carry them. From the sheltering palm leaves above, you will weave a sturdy pack with two comfortable straps. The supplies will be your strengths, talents, and personal resources.

Often, innate talents and abilities have been slumbering for long periods of time lying dormant from pressures of society, family, or your own denial of their importance. When you choose a path to consciously or unknowingly please someone else while turning away from what you feel passionate about, discontentment follows. Turning away from self-knowledge and inner guidance under pressures of judgment and conformity washes away the expression of your true self and your destiny. Rekindling self-knowledge uncovers vast personal strengths, self-confidence, and creativity.

In using Creative Intelligence, your creative process begins with the expression of your unique talents and abilities. Uncovering personal assets stirs your creative confidence and sparks the creative connection that will lead you to fulfillment.

During my first session with clients I ask them to list their greatest strengths. Usually, they can list maybe three in the first session. Over the course of our journey together the list grows and grows until at least an entire page is filled. Why? Their true self is surfacing as we lift away the ideals of others, pressure, stress, and misguided beliefs I call *untruths*. Untruths comprise a definition of self-meaning imposed by others that conflict with the congruency of your true self. They are untrue to your soul and self-limiting. I look for untruths within the language a client uses, such as *I can't*, or *I shouldn't*, and search for the connecting experiences that somehow untruthfully reinforce a *limiting self-belief*, while at the same time searching for experiences that contradict the limited self-belief and support their *true self*.

Think of what you enjoy, what gives you pleasure, and you will find the keys to unlock your talents and abilities. Enjoyment and pleasure guide you to what connects you to your creative self, and encourages you to embrace it and recognize your own talents.

"THE CREATIVE MIND PLAYS WITH THE OBJECTS IT LOVES." ~ CARL JUNG

Our Journey: Connecting With Our Physical Self

Your physical being allows you to take your journey, and concretely turns your creative ideas into fruition. Your body can also take away from your creativity, impeding the flow of life if you are not in tune with your physical self. How can you create a beautiful masterpiece if you are physically exhausted?

Your body is like a tuning fork that allows the energy of life to flow through and stimulate you. Allowing space for the connection with your breath strengthens your core and conditioning. Have you ever gone for a walk to "clear your head"? I often will save a concept I am thinking about for the gym or a long walk, and during my workout I focus on my thoughts while connecting with my breath. By the end of my workout I have gained great clarity.

Connecting with your physical self can put new perspectives in play, create possibilities of relief, and generate creative answers. The physical aspect of your journey clears the way for your creative connection by removing and relieving the congestion of accumulated stress and imbalance.

"WHERE THE SPIRIT DOES NOT CONNECT WITH THE HAND, THERE IS NO ART." ~ LEONARDO DA VINCI

Our Compass: Alignment of Our Spiritual Self

Your physical self allows the flow of life to run through you and generates spiritual energy. Spiritual energy creates movement, guidance, and direction.

Along a stretch of the 10 Highway in California you will pass a "herd" of windmills beautifully aligned with each other. There are rows and rows of these towering, white windmills gently turning in time with one another as they face the breezes that pass through the mountain valleys. I always imagine we are like the three-bladed windmills, separate yet connected with the three aspects of our beings turning into the flow of life.

Your physical self holds the elements of your spiritual self, emotional self, and your intellectual self, just as the tall cylinder base of the windmill supports the wind-catching blades. There are some windmills that happen to face away from the direction of the wind, and as you can imagine, they remain perfectly still. Some partially face the wind, reminding me of individuals who painfully creak forward in life. All of these windmills, whether still or in full movement are connected to an energy generator that shares the created power with others. Of course, those facing the wind produce the most energy. So if you direct yourself to the flow of life like the windmills facing the wind, you too will enjoy your fulfillment of movement and give energy to others.

Christianity describes this direction as accepting the Holy Spirit, which is needed to do God's will. Accepting the energy of life is as simple as believing its existence. We all have a spiritual compass that instinctively guides us to our creative destiny. As you move through your map, the compass of life will grow stronger as you push away the ideas of others and awaken all aspects of your being to sense the creative energy that continually flows around and through you.

"TO WALK WITHOUT THE SPIRIT IS TO WALK WITHOUT WISDOM."
~ EPHESIANS 5:17

The Temple: Inspiration

As you embark on your journey, your steps are guided by the beating of your heart and you become completely connected with your breath. Your internal compass assures you that you are traveling in the right direction and with this knowledge you travel well. Your pack of supplies continually fills as you journey on your path, and this knowledge gives you security. With your compass, your pack of supplies, and your treasured map, fear is no longer with you. Judgment is no longer with you. The voices of others are no longer with you. You become completely centered and balanced listening to the music of life as you are guided to a place filled with inspiration.

The first destination on your map resembles an ancient structure. Reaching that goal, there before you stands a temple. Below the balcony entrance, rows of natives sing. Within the harmony beats the rhythm of life that connects us all. Their songs fill the air with spirit and hope, energizing every particle of air. To breathe in the air awakens your soul.

People are all pulled to "temples" in our modern world with the connective experiences in churches, musical concerts, group prayer, historical sites, plays, and movies. When I am in church I hear my soul so loudly when we all pray together that tears come to my eyes. I can feel the spiritual energy as others speak their praise and prayer in unison with mine. Your soul's voice is unique to you, but also universally connected with all others, and we are all drawn together to absorb each other's energy and in turn awaken what is uniquely within each of us.

"...POETS...CREATE FROM THE VERY DEPTHS OF THE COLLECTIVE UNCONSCIOUS, VOICING ALOUD WHAT OTHERS ONLY DREAM." ~ CARL JUNG

The Legend: Dreams

Glimpses of the wisdom of our souls surface in our dreams through visual archetypes. The genesis of this chapter came entirely to me within the story line of one dream filtered through my own personal meaning of Creative Intelligence. The visual form within my dream of the sun's penetrating rays of warm light piercing the isolation of the island represents how hope continues to rise to us each day to enlighten our path to creative fulfillment, to create and aspire us to greatness, and to live congruently with our soul.

The form of water largely represents life in dreams. When you dream of a body of water, you are likely dreaming of the state of your life. Water was ever present within my dream, around the image of the island, pooling in tides, filtering through the palm leaves like drops from the Heavens. The energy of life continues to flow all around you and sustains your existence. The peaking life force of the ocean's waves lapping against the shore represents the opportunity for changing and artistically creating your own life.

Dreams comprise the legend of your map and lead to endless creative options guided by your soul. Dreams reflect deep personal meaning and give invaluable clues to unleashing unique abilities, talents, and desires. Your dreams are manifestations of your mind creating solutions to struggles, providing you with inspiration, and carefully unlocking your soul's knowledge. By attending to the archetypical knowledge presented in your dreams you can channel the awesome wisdom of the soul into creative imagination.

> "THE SOUL OF MAN IS IMMORTAL AND IMPERISHABLE."
> ~ PLATO, THE REPUBLIC, 360BC

Inspiration to Realization

Bringing the knowledge of the soul to conscious awareness generates inspiration. You are driven to create and express what is uniquely within you. Utilizing your creative imagination to generate useful innovative solutions for life requires logical refinement or reason.

Inspiration to realization reflects your ability to use and express your Creative Intelligence, to use your conscious intellect and your unconscious guide simultaneously. Accessing the skill of Creative Intelligence requires *Divergent Thinking,* which produces many answers to the same question, as opposed to seeing only one correct answer or maybe none at all.

Individuals who are considered "creative" are defined by their ability to see connections between seemingly unrelated elements. The great inventors, Nobel Prize winners, artists, philosophers, and entrepreneurs of our time and before are inspiring examples of the intellectual ability to transform inspirational ideas into reality.

Thomas Edison spoke of engaging in active or lucid dreaming techniques as he refined his inspirations to inventions. Focusing on his thoughts, he would rhythmically rock in his rocking chair while holding a small ball in each hand. As he fell asleep, the sound of the balls hitting the ground would jar him awake. He would mentally recall the unconscious knowledge and then intellectually refine his inspiration for inventions by gauging the usefulness applied to his work in progress.

By actively engaging your soulful knowledge, physically allowing the connection through relaxation, and maintaining an openness to divergent thinking, you can acquire the ability to access and logically refine your inspirations. You can then implement your creative ideas into action and invent your daily existence.

"WE MUST, IN THE NEXT PLACE, INVESTIGATE THE SUBJECT OF THE DREAM, AND FIRST INQUIRE TO WHICH OF THE FACULTIES OF THE SOUL IT PRESENTS ITSELF, FOR EXAMPLE WHETHER THE AFFECTION IS ONE WHICH PERTAINS TO THE FACULTY OF INTELLIGENCE OR TO THAT OF SENSE-PERCEPTION; FOR THESE ARE THE ONLY FACULTIES WITHIN US BY WHICH WE ACQUIRE KNOWLEDGE." ~ ARISTOTLE, ON DREAMS, 350 BC

The Field of Poppies: Emotional Presence

Returning to your map, filled with spirit you depart through the marble columns of the temple and look at your surroundings. Self-knowledge fills you with trust and direction. Light bounces off every leaf like fairy dust sprinkled from the Divine. The beauty of everything stimulates all of the senses, bringing a heightened state of experience as you become aware of yourself.

A field of poppies with every color ever created appears before the temple. As you move through the poppies they feel like strips of velvet brushing against your shins. You notice every shape and texture. You are completely in the present and feel the tingling of your senses awakening with every step.

Maintaining emotional presence allows you to push away regrets from the past and avoid anxieties of the future. Learning to remain emotionally present to channel the creative energy requires trust. Trust in your abilities, self-knowledge, and your destined path guided by your map. If you live in a place of trust, rather than hearing regrets of the past, you will peer back at your journey and notice accomplishment. You will look ahead on your journey and see faith.

We all have the capability of experiencing emotional presence in life. A hiker atop a pinnacle, a writer engaged in fluid thought, a mother enjoying a child's hug, a husband lost in the touch of his wife, a moment when nothing else matters but enjoyment and experience. Emotional presence is a celebration of life, self-awareness, and gratitude. With emotional presence you can trust to be completely in the present and enjoy every sense of your being aligning with the energy of creation, enjoy the beauty of life, and create inspiring wonders in your everyday world.

"I CAN FEEL GUILTY ABOUT THE PAST, APPREHENSIVE ABOUT THE FUTURE, BUT ONLY IN THE PRESENT CAN I ACT." ~ ABRAHAM MASLOW

The Hidden Treasure:
Unlocking Your Creative Potential

Serenity, peace, balance, simplicity. Our rainbow carpet of poppies ends at an expansive marsh as wide as the eye can see. The scent of the ocean approaches with a fine mist. You scan the shoreline and notice a bright reflection signaling an object hidden within the sand. Could this be the treasure of the map? The brightness of the reflection shields your view and you drop to your knees to uncover the object. A treasure box built of gold and lined with brass nails antiqued with time and the elements lies loosely in the sand. As you lift the box, sand pours from the crevices. A large key-shaped lock, polished and shiny, rests where the lid meets the box.

Your inner voice speaks to you, "just lift the lid." And you listen. The lid glides open and light pours from the contents of the treasure. Wonder fills you as you look inside. At the bottom of the treasure box, a mirror stares back at you, reflecting your deepest treasure...*You. You* are the treasure of the map. You hold the key to unlock your creative potential through the process of integrating self-awareness, self-gratitude, self-growth, and the understanding of your own significance and your connection with the universe.

The authentic integration of your journey unlocks your Creative Intelligence through the process of *Creative Convergence*, where the intellect and self-actualization merge with your desire to be unique. This convergence of your whole self provides the ability to push away conformity, honor your inner voice, and express yourself to your fullest to reach a place of innovation. *Creative Convergence* can be described as a state of complete balance, a peak experience when all your senses align with your physical, spiritual, emotional, and intellectual aspects of self.

> "YOUR VISION WILL BECOME CLEAR ONLY WHEN YOU CAN LOOK INSIDE YOUR OWN HEART. WHO LOOKS OUTSIDE DREAMS. WHO LOOKS INSIDE AWAKENS." ~ CARL JUNG

The Shore: Creative Perspective

You have arrived. The other side of the island greets you with the calmness and serenity of a tranquil bay. The cool pale blue of the sky peeks through the stratus of the pink and orange clouds, and the sun melts into the sea. The moon will soon appear to signal the evening's arrival. You know and understand the order of the universe. Your experiences of your journey have collected here and stir with ocean breezes. Your mind moves to a new level, accessing the deep collective unconscious, your personal spirit, and your physical resources, and pools into your thoughts, touching every aspect of your created beliefs.

Your vision expands to take in the panoramic shoreline. The edges of the island, once defining and encapsulating, seem to melt into the sea. You recognize new possibilities. Within the unlimited possibilities you find your *Creative Perspective*, an awakening and expansion of creative potential, confidence, and concentration.

Creative Perspective brings order and structure to your imagination and ideas through a process of decoding thoughts— visual representations—and comparing them to past experiences you have integrated into your personal meaning. A self-meaning that is congruent with your soul, free from untruths, and free to create your *true self*. With *Creative Perspective* you see through the eyes of your true self and trust in your ability to use your map to Creative Intelligence, rather than hindering your creativity by restricting your self-beliefs.

> "I SAW THE ANGEL IN THE MARBLE AND I CARVED UNTIL I SET HIM FREE."
> ~ MICHELANGELO

The Horizon: A Preferred Life

Facing the rippling pools of water left by the receding tides of the ocean, the horizon paints a majestic vision of creative options beyond the marsh. Where fear may have stepped in before, now security and trust are with you in the present. On your journey, you have gathered inspiration, trust, and security to use Creative Intelligence to masterfully create your life.

Through the intellectual process of evaluation you are able to gauge the usefulness of your inspirational travels. To apply this evaluation effectively in your life, you must have a goal that exists in congruence with your true self. Defining goals creates a vision of what I name *A Preferred Life*. The vision of your preferred life provides you with the canvas to paint your inspiration.

Life Coaches largely assist others in the construction of meaningful and fulfilling goals. By constructing goals congruent with your personal meaning you become *intrinsically motivated* to successfully complete your creative goals. You are motivated from within rather than by outside rewards. Individuals who are intrinsically motivated are much more likely to achieve their vision, reach a place of satisfaction, and gain contentment with their accomplishments.

Intrinsic motivation drives people through the rewards of personal enjoyment and accomplishment. Hobbies and art are examples of activities where we are intrinsically motivated to engage in activities for the mere pleasure or sense of accomplishment it brings. By constructing your vision of *A Preferred Life* to be congruent with what passionately drives you, what brings meaning and enjoyment to your life, you automatically shift your motivational drive to internal rather than external. The reward becomes the process of continually creating meaningful goals and enjoying the journey—enjoying, creating, contributing to your own personal growth as well as inspiring others. Keeping your vision on the horizon before you maintains your path and keeps you steady even in the face of challenges.

You can create your own vision of *A Preferred Life* by tapping into your soulful self, achieving balance, and heightening your personal experience outlined within the journey of this Map to Creative Intelligence. Your vision of *A Preferred Life* will continue to change as you continue to add detail and richness to your journey in life, creating beautiful masterpieces each day of your life.

"THE INDIVIDUAL IS THUS BOTH THE PICTURE AND THE ARTIST."
~ ALFRED ADLER

The Boat: Support

As you face the vastness of the shore, the sun dips into the horizon. The eve of creation rests before you. Soft light filters through the peaks of the ocean carrying hope and faith continuously toward the shore. The soothing rhythm of the ocean claps against the shore and quietly recedes, leaving pools of the tide to collect the remaining rays of the sun.

You focus your attention to a rocking form shadowed against the sunset. You recognize the mast of sail. There is a boat, gently pulling against its anchor, eager to fulfill its created destiny and set sail into the current of the ocean. The boat is your support, a vehicle for creating. As you value and trust your unique expression of your self you will seek those who encourage your creativity—a Coach, a friend, a teacher, a parent, a *supporter*.

Although the boat appears to you at the end of your journey, the boat can also be the beginning. You create your own support through your own investigation, research, and will. Creating your own support generates empowerment, confidence, and creative energy. Uncover your vehicle for creating through reading, learning, exploring, engaging in new experiences, and surrounding yourself with those who encourage and support you. As you build your own support, work also to create an environment of support around you.

> "BELIEVE ONLY WHAT YOU YOURSELF TEST AND JUDGE TO BE TRUE."
> ~ BUDDHA

Setting Sail: Intelligent Creation

Through choice you move your creative self into conscious action. You are the navigator of your life. You are accountable for your creations. You can choose to follow your creative map or continue the suppression of your full self and turn your island paradise into desolation. Understand that you were born for greatness, meaning, and purpose. Utilize your Creative Intelligence, not only for your own self-actualization and fulfillment, but to discover your greater purpose and contribution to others. What does your inner voice guide you to do? Listen and follow...explore and discover...research and support...*Intelligently Create*.

To optimize your potential is to create. To endure is the intellectual decision to create in the face of challenge through choice, will, and determination. I urge you to endure, to persevere, and to be uniquely you. The desire to share your creation with others brings ambition, satisfaction, and future inspiration. The cycle of creation exists in everything around you—jump in and set sail.

The Map to Creative Intelligence guides you to your own place of creation, seamlessly merging your creativity and intellect into one experience. Using Creative Intelligence, you will sail through life optimizing your creative power with reason and passion. Your *passion* will provide the fuel to propel you toward your Preferred Life, your *reason* will steer you in the right direction. And so you engage the flow of life and the elation of existence. The boat will carry you, but you will navigate its path, carving into the depths of the ocean of life as you use empowerment to set sail. Using the flow of life to propel your sails, your spiritual compass to light your path, and your intellect to make wise decisions, you will *create* a remarkable journey of fulfillment with the ultimate balance of your soul guiding your reason and your passion.

"YOUR REASON AND YOUR PASSION ARE THE RUDDER AND THE SAILS OF YOUR SEAFARING SOUL." ~ KHALIL GIBRAN, THE PROPHET

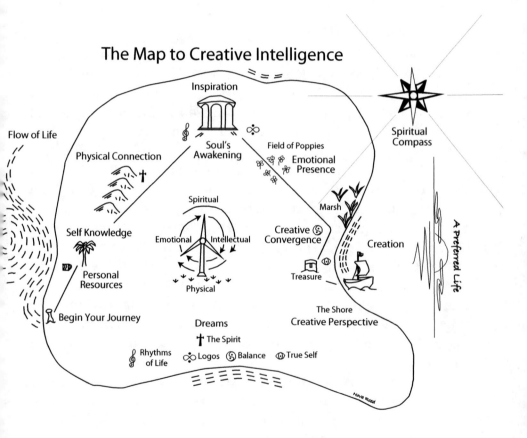

The Map to Creative Intelligence

About
Nova Reed

Nova Reed, M.A., Life Coach, founded Step Stones For Life as a venue dedicated to helping others create a Preferred Life through the creation of meaningful goals, balance, health, and creativity. Nova developed the proven coaching strategies of Step Stones For Life defining the universal steps needed to discover and strengthen the path to fulfillment, incorporating her background in psychology and health. Nova received her B.A. in Psychology and Social Behavior with an emphasis in Health Psychology from the University of California Irvine. She furthered her education and training at Pepperdine University Graduate School of Education and Psychology, receiving her Master's Degree in Clinical Psychology with an emphasis in Marriage and Family Therapy.

Nova defines her work as a collaborative journey with her clients, with the belief the individual holds their own key to success through the integration of their strengths and abilities congruent with their soul. In developing her model of coaching, Nova found the element of creativity to be a key component to an individual's ability to generate positive solutions, create goals, and visualize their future. Nova's strong commitment to her faith speaks through her writing and heightens her ability to connect with her clients.

The link between our physical being, our spiritual self, and our emotional intellect comprises the key philosophy behind the life-changing techniques of Step Stones For Life. One cannot exist without the other. How we nurture and care for ourselves affects how well we thrive and cope in the world. This mind-body connection has been explored for centuries and in today's world of heightened stress, multiple demands, and high pressure, finding time and the avenue to renew your physical self, connect with your soul, and discover your ability to remain balanced even in high pressure situations is vital to health, well-being, and relationships. When our physical-spiritual-emotional self remains balanced, our mental outlook, health, productivity, and personal relationships improve. Step Stones For Life coaching strategies address the whole individual, with the understanding that balance, harmony, and a complete existence leads to contentment, stress reduction, and inner peace.

"We seek to discover ourselves by looking to others, we measure success by the attainment of things, we uncover love by the treatment of others, and yet feel empty. We quest for answers, for happiness, for joy, and yet sadness remains inescapable. By chance, or through investigation, we find a helper, a guide, a mentor, a Coach, who sweeps away the cobwebs and brightens our vision. She holds in her palm a plan for our fulfillment, and sees through her eyes all of our superb qualities and talents. She heightens our beliefs, our confidence, and our commitment to ourselves. We find trust, compassion, and purpose with meaningful passion. The world seems clear and we recognize a path for which we have forgotten...The Path to Fulfillment. We smile as the warm sun sparkles off the gleaming edges, pulling us in to take our first steps. How remarkable, we realize that our path was right before us blocked by the conditioning and suppression of ourselves."

~ Nova Reed, M.A., Life Coach

Begin your journey with Step Stones For Life. Improve the quality of your life, your relationships, productivity, and find meaningful success. Unblock factors that keep you from living the life you desire. The life you have only imagined is just steps away.

Step Stones For Life is located in Orange County, California, providing creative life coaching for individuals, couples, children, and businesses. In-person, telephone coaching, and speaking engagements available. To contact Nova, email nova@stepstonesforlife.com, call 949-858-2442, toll free: 1-877-484-LIFE, or visit www.stepstonesforlife.com.

Awakening the Creative Intelligence of Your Soul Through the Connection with God's Spirit

By Kathryn Bonner

The Holy Spirit's Guidance is Paramount in Creative Intelligence!

When I was a young girl, my friends and I would lay in the grass, flat on our backs gazing up at the wispy clouds blowing ever so slowly into different shapes. We'd point up to the clouds and ask one another, "Do you see the poodle? Do you see the airplane? …the witch? …the high heel shoes? …the car? …the camel? …the pelican?" The clouds seemed to be there specifically for our entertainment. We'd stay there for hours on beautiful days. Lying there with my friends, we'd have deep, profound conversations. Even in our youth, we knew that our Creator was amazing. Looking up at the vast never-ending blue and white puffs in the sky, we'd ask powerfully felt questions, wondering, "How in the world did God form the earth and everything in it?"

There was a huge honeysuckle bush that lined an entire fence, and while we were lying there sky gazing we'd pick the golden- yellow, trumpet-shaped flowers. We'd look for the little green stem on the end and pull it like a thread through the flower, dragging the tiny dab of sugary sweet syrup to our lips, taking great pleasure from the taste of the honey. We wondered how the pleasing syrup got in the beautiful honeysuckle flower. Again we were amazed with the Lord's Creative Intelligence. We took delight in the wonder of it all. As we surveyed our surroundings, the talk would inevitably shift to God.

As we continued looking up at the clouds, our ears heard the buzzing sound of a bumblebee, and we'd look around in a bit of fright, our eyes following it. The bumblebee is an amazing creature. Did you know it is one of the few insects that can regulate its temperature through both solar radiation (radiant energy emitted by the sun) and through an internal mechanism of cooling from its abdomen?

We would then fix our eyes on other creatures around us. We'd pick up the doodle bugs (also known as roly-pollies, pill bugs, and armadillo bugs). These bugs have a shell-like body that can tuck and roll up for protection, which is how they got many of the names we called them. Most people think that they are insects, but they are not. They actually breathe through gills. In the tiniest little creature, there is such creativity, such beauty!

Early in my life, I became aware of the Holy Spirit through God's creation, of animals and nature, through the wind and rain, through the flowing river, through silence and through music, through laughter and tears, through joy, through relationships, through sweet aromas, sunrises and sunsets, and clouds. Ultimately, I hear and experience God through love, which I consider to be the most creative and intelligent source. I recognize that we all have unique experiences that draw us to God; this is just a fraction of my experience.

The Illumination of the Holy Spirit Powerfully Revealed...

A few years later when I was fourteen, I went to an amazing summer camp with my youth group. The week was brimming with countless new understandings of Christ. I'd never *"felt"* the powerfulness of God that way. I knew *for sure* for the first time in my life that God was *actually real*. This knowing was powerful; it was pure. The feeling I had was as though a gentle rain of grace was showering upon me, and this grace was filling my heart and soul, transforming and renewing my mind. I was experiencing an amazing love, and a new freedom. In a certain strange kind of way, I felt a *whole new earth, of form and beauty and refinement*, a new way of seeing, of feeling, of hearing. I experienced the favor and blessing of God. I cried tears of joy, tears of realization. I'll never forget the permeation of the Holy Spirit. This is the moment I chose to walk with God.

2 COR. 5:17 THEREFORE, IF ANYONE IS IN CHRIST HE IS A NEW CREATION,
THE OLD HAS GONE, THE NEW HAS COME.

At the time, I didn't know what the Word said regarding the way we are filled with the power of the Holy Spirit upon accepting Him as our Lord and savior. After this transformational week at camp, I went back to high school (to the "old earth"), trying to, and wanting to live for Him. I realized I should back away from the group with whom I had been hanging out. Changing was difficult; peer pressure is a burly thing. My parents were going through a divorce and we lived with my mother. I was defiant and acting out. I tried to detach myself from the "old group" and latch onto a new group. The old group didn't want to let me go, and the new group wasn't allowing me in. I went to my mother and told her of my need to embark on my new faith walk, explaining the circumstances to her. I needed to go to a different school. She agreed and put her dream house on the market. That was such an amazing gift my mother gave to me. Though I knew she was making a sacrifice, as an adult I appreciate it so much more. We moved, and I began my sophomore year at the new school, and adopted healthier friends and a new way of living.

Even though all of this change in my life had come about because of Him, in the process I seemed to have forgotten about my Lord. I didn't make Him the Lord and master of my life. I was however, hanging out with better kids, staying out of trouble while having lots of fun.

Oh, I prayed every now and then, and thought about God primarily when I had a need. But I wasn't really focused on, or into God any more. I believed in God, but wasn't living my life for Him. At that time my life felt aimless. I didn't have a clear purpose. I didn't have the calm and the peace and the joy. I didn't have the confidence. I didn't have clarity. I felt empty because of the way I had strayed.

At age nineteen in 1981, I became pregnant with my daughter Tabitha. Fear and uncertainty with what to do ensued. Following the advice of my parents, I felt that I had to marry her father. We married on Valentines Day, 1982. I turned twenty in June and my beautiful baby girl was born in July. We had our second beauty, Kellie Ann, in 1985. The marriage lasted seven years. A few years before the marriage was over, I again sought out my Lord.

A New Beginning...

I longed for the Lord to be a continual presence in my life. I had a *real need* for Him and began to find Him in the small "ah ha's" of living. It was refreshing and it was renewal, it was joyful, it was real, it was heaven here on earth. I began to experience His love for me in many unexpected ways. I was in connection with a great church, had been provided with coaches and mentors, and a great job. The Lord began to position godly girlfriends in my life. They prayed with me and for me. His presence around me was unmistakable, unwavering, and unshakable.

I was divorced. Just me and my two little girls on our own were making it with God's help. We were going to church together each Sunday. I wanted them to be on familiar, intimate terms with the Lord growing up. I wanted to be reconnected to the love I'd known in Christ Jesus at the age of fourteen. We went on our church search. However, looking for the perfect church for all three of us wasn't happening quickly. We persisted until we found it. We were beginning our new walk of faith. Little did I know where this walk was going to take me. But God in his Creative Intelligence knew.

Connecting to Holy Spirit to Awaken Your Own Creative Intelligence

When I think about "Creative Intelligence" I think of God, as the Holy Spirit. God is the definitive, The Great Creator, and the Greatest of all Intelligence. This scripture comes to mind...

> DO YOU NOT KNOW? HAVE YOU NOT HEARD? THE LORD IS THE EVERLASTING GOD, THE CREATOR OF THE ENDS OF THE EARTH. HE WILL NOT GROW TIRED OR WEARY, AND HIS UNDERSTANDING NO ONE CAN FATHOM. ~ ISAIAH 40:28 NLT

Clearly, we are to be in connection and awakened to what our amazing creator of unfathomable intelligence has for us. God is our reason for being. I marvel at His creation, and holy mysteries.

What does having an "Awakened Life" or "Holy Spirit-connected life" mean? It means to live wholly holy. Don't mistake this way of living as "having to be perfect." For me, it means to be completely in step with the Holy Spirit, to make a choice for Christ. Within that choice is an amazing freedom. He carries our burdens, instills us with His Holy Spirit. This is amazing love. This is the ultimate in Creative Intelligence.

Keeping in step with the Spirit takes active concentration, commitment, and discipline. Unfortunately, many of us pay attention to so many other things that keep us from living and walking with the Holy Spirit. One obstacle is pride, which C. S. Lewis says, "is spiritual cancer that eats up the very possibility of love, or contentment, or even common sense." Then there is ego (a friend of mine states that ego is an acronym for Edging God Out) and judgment. We must tune them out in order to listen only to the Holy Spirit of God.

Through prayer, I hear and experience God's guidance every day. Have you ever said or done things that you were simply guided to do? Things that you've never known anyone else to do, things that no one has ever told you to do—you just know that you are supposed to do it? This has happened many times in my life.

I love the way music speaks to my soul, even though I am not one who can sing or play an instrument. When I was pregnant with my first child, I was listening to some music when the Lord guided me to wrap headphones around my belly. So I turned the music on low so that my baby girl was able to hear the music in the womb. I know I looked peculiar walking around with headphones strapped around me, but both of us enjoyed the beautiful songs of praise. I did it again during my second pregnancy. The result? Both of my daughters have the most beautiful voices, and can harmonize together in such a way that it brings tears to my eyes, causing me to experience God through them in what I hear.

In addition, my daughters have an uncanny ability to hear the sounds of a cello, a flute, a guitar, an obo, the violin, and many other sounds of music. We can be in a loud, crowded restaurant and they will say to me, "Mom, can you hear the flute playing?" I will say, "Oh, there's music playing?" I'd then try to tune out all of the other things and hear the music. So it is with God: we have to tune out the things that keep us from hearing Him.

Another experience with the Holy Spirit, hearing God... I've never had any aspirations to write a book. Recently I had a profound experience. I was sitting on the sofa in the den watching TV. All of a sudden, a list of chapter titles flooded my mind. I literally ran into my office and grabbed my prayer journal and began writing them all down as they came rushing in. There were twenty-six chapter titles, and amazingly I knew what was to be written in every single chapter. Another thing I found to be remarkable was that they were given to me in perfect speed—no faster than I could write so that I wouldn't forget any of them. When God gives He gives so perfectly! I stood there awestruck, staring at the page of chapter titles. I was overwhelmed by this occurrence. I was thrilled, and yet it felt daunting and beyond my capabilities.

In retrospect, I looked at this as my "burning bush event." It was as though God had spoken to me telling me to write a book for Him. I think about how Moses felt when the Lord gave him his task. I felt overwhelmed, unable, unqualified, and unworthy. Because I felt all of those things, I set my prayer journal on the shelf in my office and let it sit there for a few months.

The Lord would nudge me and cause me to remember the chapter titles He'd given me. I felt incapable and incompetent to attempt to tackle the writing of the book. I recognized that God was calling me back to it, encouraging me to accept the assignment. Eventually, I came to terms with the idea that it's okay to aspire to do what He's called you to. I felt as though I didn't deserve to do this. God helped me come to terms with that thought. He wanted me to exercise my faith, trust Him, embrace it, and experience the joy rather than the fear of it. I began to consider thoughts like "Maybe I can do this. Maybe I really did hear Him ask me to do this? Surely, He will continue to guide me through it. He has always guided me before, why would he stop now?" I thought, "Kathryn, you've always been the one to step out in faith, allowing the Holy

Spirit, rather than fear, to lead you." I thought, "As a Life Coach, I always encourage my clients to walk into whatever it is that God is calling them to, always the first one to say 'go for it' when they have felt afraid, especially when they knew it was God who was calling them to something." Then I reminded myself: "Practice what you preach girl! Step out in faith; take the risk. Do it for God."

It's been said—and I believe this with my whole heart—we speak to God with every word and breath that we release. And with each and every breath we breathe in, He makes Himself known to us. After all, He is the breath of life. We are never apart or separated from God, although we can miss "hearing him speak to us" if we are not tuned in to His message. Too often, we tune Him out, like so many other things in our lives.

He doesn't always have to speak in audible sounds. He gives us great and small signs all around us. In fact, the quietness of the sunsets have been "speaking to my soul" a lot lately. My husband Bruce and I have just moved back to the Austin area and we find ourselves awestruck at the beauty of the hill country. We just recently purchased a hammock and have it in the backyard. I lay in it and read, bathing in the warmth of the sun, listening to the birds, and soft sounds of the wind in the trees.

We have a little roadrunner family of three living next door. Bruce was on the side of the house repositioning the sprinkler when one of the roadrunners scampered up and stood in the spray of the water. He stared straight at Bruce and stretched out his wings, and fanned them open wide so that the water would sprinkle over him! Bruce stood in amazement, soaking in the joy of it all. Holy Spirit of majesty, fun, and love, all at once. A charming gift from God!

Bruce and I drive through the hills and we have found a spot in which we love to park high on a hill overlooking the city. We go there to pray and experience His majesty, His beautiful creation. Our souls are fed by soaking in the sunsets, breathing in the beauty, meditating on the golden, purple, and pink hues that are incredibly gorgeous and absolutely breathtaking. There are winding oak trees placed perfectly in the landscaped canvas. The stunning silhouettes of the trees grace me with their age and wisdom. They are large and sturdy and elegant. There are cacti and large boulders, laced with wispy vines and flowers that smell so sweet, allowing me to take pleasure in the beauty the earth provides. In those times, I experience the power of the connection of the Holy Spirit. But these are not the only moments I receive the Creative Intelligence of God. In every moment of every day, I see, hear, smell, taste and experience the beauty of His creation.

Consciously Choosing a Life in Connection with Jesus, the One Who Gives Us His Holy Spirit

To embrace the majesty of all that the Holy Spirit provides, I have to first choose to do so. This is a conscious choice for me. I know the effects of what my days can be when I have not invited the Holy Spirit into my day, my life, first thing in the morning. When I allow myself to be hurried by what the day has in store for me, I am the one who is adversely affected. Acknowledging the Lord through prayer allows me to be able to experience His presence fully, and opens me to His love, and my experiences reflect the love of Christ.

As I reflect back on the days when it did not come naturally, I want to say that it doesn't necessarily happen over night. It truly is a choice, and does take effort, commitment, hope, and, of course, faith. There were many days when I would pull the kneeler down in the pew, and on bended knee I would almost beg God not to let me forget about Him when I would walk out the church doors. And then, the very moment I'd walk out, what did I do? I left it all behind me.

When you ask for something, you have to own it. God does not forget you; you forget God. While I would pray the words, "Please don't let me forget you," He was not going to force me to remember Him. What a great lesson for me. It takes consistency, repetition, and belief. With time, it becomes a beautiful relationship. Our Lord desires to have a relationship with you; He is a relational God. This is why relationships are vital to us as human beings.

The Holy Spirit Works in Mysterious Ways—A New Beginning...

Isn't it amazing how our Lord brings us many new beginnings in this wonderful life? I was not dating nor was I interested in dating, because of my two little girls, Tabitha, age six, and Kellie Ann, four. I wasn't going to bring men in and out of my life. I was happy with it being we girls. We had great fun. I felt complete with them. I felt like it would just be the three of us from here on out and had peace about that. God had other plans—I was set up on a blind date, and met Bruce.

During our dating, we really got to know each other over the phone. We talked for hours; he'd pray with me, and dialogue, talk of our dreams, and of what God wanted for us.

The way God gives us new beginnings at different stages of our lives is interesting. Oh, how I give thanks for this love of my life! Bruce and I met on March 29, 1989. He proposed in June, and we were married on August 26, 1989. He was called to the ministry, and I'm grateful to be a part of his calling and his ministry.

Many Years Later, Another New Beginning—Empty Nesters...

We lived in a charming, out-of-the-way, small Texas town in which my husband was the pastor of a church. We loved the people there. It was a truly wonderful place. My career as Vice President of CARES By Apartment Life, a nationwide non-profit Christian organization causes me to travel extensively. The cities of focus in my portfolio are Houston, Austin, San Antonio, and Atlanta. Traveling to those cities was squandering away too many hours in a day, causing me to have to stay in hotels. Bruce didn't like the hours I was spending on the road or the days apart that we had to endure, and quite frankly, neither did I. In February of 2005, we began to pray about the opportunity to reside in one of the three Texas cities that were in my portfolio. God commenced to lead us, the way Holy Spirit always does when we walk with Him.

We began to examine different church newsletters in the Austin and San Antonio area. We looked for those that we knew were either going to be searching for a priest or were currently without a priest. Of the churches we looked at, we were continuously guided back to Christ Episcopal Church (CEC) in Cedar Park. They'd been without a priest for approximately two years. The Spirit continued to draw us back to this church in many different ways.

In reading the church newsletters on line, we began to be acutely aware that the Spirit was moving in this community, and in the people. It was exciting to witness from a distance.

In early March I went on-line and did a Google search for homes in Cedar Park and Leander. I clicked on the very first listing. The screen was slow to divulge the picture of the real estate agent. As the screen began to reveal the eyes of the agent, I recognized them. I called to Bruce, "I recognize these eyeballs! They are Carolyn's! I didn't know she was back in real estate." I have known Carolyn for many years; in fact I met her before I knew Bruce, and before she knew her husband Lou. After Bruce and I married, while Bruce was in seminary, he worked for Lou. After Carolyn and Lou married, all four of us became friends. Eventually, we had moved away, losing track of them.

When we saw her sky blue, almond-shaped eyes on the web, Bruce said, "That's who we are using. Let's call right now!" We made an appointment to look for a house the first of April.

The moment we walked into the first model home, we felt like we were home. Bruce and I prayed, and we put our money down, selected the lot and proceeded to build. The house was slotted to be ready for occupancy the first part of August. Lou and Carolyn were a bit stunned that we put our money down so quickly, knowing that we had not spoken to the Bishop or to anyone at the church.

In June, we had an appointment to visit with the Bishop's office. We explained the situation with my job and the need to live in one of the cities within my portfolio. They understood and were going to check into what churches would be available. At that meeting, we asked them about CEC, and he point blank told us that they were not ready for a priest. We never told them that we had a house being built, not wanting anyone to feel manipulated into anything. We were trusting God.

Two days after that meeting, CEC called the Bishops office at the diocese and informed them that they were ready for a priest. They in turn told CEC about us, and it went from there. Of course, we never revealed to CEC that we were already having our house built until it was a "done deal" for the same reason we never told the office of the Bishop. It was our little secret. The only ones who knew were Lou and Carolyn, our two daughters, and of course God. It was such fun, and so inspiring to experience faith in action. Talk about the ultimate in Creative Intelligence, the Holy Spirit.

From My Heart to Your Heart...

I want for you to be in connection with the Lord, the giver of life, who stretched out his arms on the cross, and offered himself, a perfect sacrifice for you and the whole world, so that you would have life everlasting.

He has joy for you, plans for you to prosper and to love, even in the midst of struggle. I want to give you hope and joy in your journey. The choice to live in every moment with love, faith, and glorious expectation is mine and yours. Don't let anything or anyone stop you from living in the glory that the Holy Spirit provides.

For those of you who have dreams, keep dreaming. Push beyond the limits of your comfort zone. Do you realize where those dreams come from? Do you trust where they originate? Step out in faith, don't just sit there sitting on your dream, embrace it. Love it, and live it!

What are you doing with your mind? Which way are you choosing to live your life? What thoughts, what character do you long for? Be transformed by the renewing of your mind.

Romans 12:2 reads: Do not be conformed to this world (this age), [fashioned after and adapted to its external, superficial customs], but be transformed (changed) by the [entire] renewal of your mind [by its new ideals and its new attitude], so that you may prove [for yourselves] what is the good and acceptable and perfect will of God, even the thing that is good and acceptable and perfect [in His sight for you]. (Amplified version)

As a Life Coach, I encourage my clients to begin praying about the plan that the Lord has, pray about the choices you make and why you make them.

My prayer for you is to Awaken your Spirit, transform your life into a breathtaking and joyous, Holy Spirit life. Live for God, because He lives for you. I know this to be true!

"If we live by the Spirit, let us also be guided by the Spirit."
~ Gal. 5:25

About
Kathryn Bonner

Kathryn Bonner believes in walking and living in step with the Holy Spirit. Having a passion for coaching, Kathryn Bonner founded Awakenings Life Coaching and Consulting. Her prayer and dream is to bring about transformation in the lives of those she coaches. Innately, everyone yearns for a fulfilling life, one of meaning and full of purpose. Unfortunately, many people just don't quite know how to live that life. When her clients feel they are sleep walking through life, Kathryn feels honored and privileged to walk along side them and aid in their Awakening.

Kathryn's discovery of the value of coaching came when her own coach helped her propel her life, transforming her and helping in her own Awakening. Having support as you walk your path helps you become connected and sure of what you are to be doing with your life.

Kathryn's coaching helps you discover *you*. Co-actively, you will face fears, step out in faith, view things from new or different perspectives, experience attitudinal shifts, and set and achieve life long goals. Kathryn brings keen intuition, enthusiasm, humor, and love to every coaching session. What clients are saying:

"Coaching empowers me to move from awareness to achievement and supports me through the journey. Kathryn is a caring person who makes each individual feel unique, special, and capable of achieving his/her higher purpose. I have awakened to my God-given gifts and passion. If you are ready to make a change, I recommend coaching to provide focus, direction, and validation during the change process. In particular, I recommend Kathryn Bonner as a coach because of her own passion for personal development and purpose." ~ E.M.H.

"The coaching I received from Kathryn Bonner is a truly amazing and life-changing experience. Her insightful questions and caring demeanor

enabled me to reflect at a very deep level on the issues and challenges I was facing. Kathryn's coaching approach had a powerful energizing and spiritual affect upon my soul. Her coaching was like a brilliant ray of light that melted away my external layers and enabled me to see from my heart and not just my mind. Kathryn's coaching skills are superb. She will be both a help and a blessing to anyone she coaches. ~ J. C.

Kathryn has twenty-five years of professional experience in Corporate America, with twenty years in property management. She brings that experience to her coaching practice. Kathryn is Vice President of CARES By Apartment Life, a nationwide non-profit Christian organization. Kathryn's professional experience, training, and affiliations include:

- CPCC – Certified Co-Active Coach, The Coaches Training Institute
- ICF – International Coach Federation member
- Certified Retreat Coach
- CCN – Christian Coaches Network
- BSF – Bible Study Fellowship (Completion of the seven-year course; six of those years in a leadership position.)

Kathryn is currently writing a book, developing meditation CD's, and planning Awakening Retreats for renewing the soul and creating a closer walk with God.

Kathryn was born and raised in Texas, and currently resides in the beautiful hill country of Austin. She is the daughter of a banker and an interior designer, which has enabled her to see beauty from many perspectives, especially within those she encounters. Her parents declare that the Sunday Kathryn was born, she came into the world with smiling eyes!

Kathryn is married to an Episcopal priest and immensely enjoys serving with him in the church. They have two grown daughters and a son-in-law. She enjoys spending time with family and friends, laughing hard, deep conversations, traveling, reading, movies, and of course coaching, leading retreats, and writing.

To contact Kathryn, call 512-260-7775, or for more information, email AwakeningsLifeCoaching@cox.net, or visit www.AwakeningsLifeCoaching@com.